Van Buren Denslow

**A plea for the introduction of responsible government and
the representation of capital into the United States as
safeguards against communism and disunion**

Van Buren Denslow

A plea for the introduction of responsible government and the representation of capital into the United States as safeguards against communism and disunion

ISBN/EAN: 9783337229191

Printed in Europe, USA, Canada, Australia, Japan

Cover: Foto ©Suzi / pixelio.de

More available books at **www.hansebooks.com**

A PLEA FOR THE INTRODUCTION

OF

RESPONSIBLE GOVERNMENT

AND THE

REPRESENTATION OF CAPITAL

INTO THE UNITED STATES,

AS SAFEGUARDS AGAINST

COMMUNISM & DISUNION.

EXTRACT FROM DeTocqueville's "DEMOCRACY IN AMERICA."

" In that immense crowd which throngs the avenues to power in the United States, I found very few men who displayed that manly candor and masculine independence of opinion which frequently distinguished the Americans in former times, and which constitutes the leading feature in distinguished characters wheresoever they may be found. It seems at first sight as if all the minds of the Americans were formed upon one model, so accurately do they follow the same route. A stranger does indeed sometimes meet with Americans who dissent from the rigor of these formularies, with men who deplore the effects of the laws, the mutability and the ignorance of democracy—who even go so far as to observe the evil tendencies which impair the national character and to point out such remedies as it might be possible to apply. * * * but * * they hold a different language in public."

By VAN BUREN DENSLOW, LL. D.,

Late Associate Editor of the New York and Chicago Tribunes, Professor of Law in the Union College of Law, and of Political Economy in the University of Chicago.

PRINTED FOR THE AUTHOR,
By JNO. C. HUGHES, SPRINGFIELD, ILL.
1879.

RESPONSIBLE GOVERNMENT.

1. OUR LACK OF IT IN THE UNITED STATES OF AMERICA, AND HOW IT MAY BE SUPPLIED.

IF any practical English or American statesman were asked to-day to point out the chief difference between the Constitution of England and that of the United States, he would probably say that it consists in the fact that in the United States, and in each of them, the executive branch of the government is elected for a fixed term of office, and during that term is independent of the legislative branch; while in England the real executive branch of the government, to-wit: the cabinet, is elected for no fixed term, and resigns either upon an adverse vote of the House of Commons, or if it calls for a popular election to test the stability of the existing House of Commons, and is beaten at the polls, then it resigns in obedience to an adverse vote of the people. In this respect, the English executive—regarding the Queen or King, of course, as a figurehead,—is flexible, and may be changed in a day, or, at most, in a month; while the American executive is inflexible, and when once elected, can not, except by impeachment for high crimes or misdemeanors, be changed in less than four years. Our legislatures, also, are inflexible, whether they represent faithfully the will of the people or not; while the English, Canadian and Australian legislatures are more flexible, since it is in the power of the executive in each of those countries to dissolve the legislature at any moment, and test, by a new election, whether the people sustain the administration, or whether they sustain the opposition legislative majority. Thus, in England, Canada and Australia the people are permitted to vote (in all important cases over which there is sufficient difference of opinions to divide parties) upon the very question on which their legislature is to act, and in time to control its action.

In America (except in certain cases wherein, by State legislation, a given question is submitted to popular vote) the people, in political campaigns, can not vote in a manner to affect any question of future action, but must

---

NOTE.—The substance of the above Chapter 1 was delivered as a lecture before the Philosophical Society of Chicago, on November 11, 1876.

simply vote an indorsement of one or the other of two sets of party candidates, and with reference to the record of the party and its candidates for the past ten, thirty or fifty years. As parties never retain their exact identity of membership or principles from one election to another, and, in the course of ten or twenty years, frequently change their general drift, bias and principles, it follows that to vote with reference to so fluctuating and uncertain an element as the past record of a political party is, of necessity, a delusive sham and swindle. It realizes, in fact, the supposed Rip Van Winkleism of the Pennsylvania Dutchman who, in the elections for Polk, Taylor and Pierce, still kept on voting for Gen. Jackson, with the slight sting to our national vanity of placing every American voter on a level with the supposed stupid Pennsylvania Dutchman. We are not only at every election voting exclusively with reference to dead issues, but it is almost a fallacy to suppose that, under our system of fixed periods of office, we can, by any possibility, vote with reference to future issues, as no man can tell, in politics, what the actual legislation of the next Congress will relate to. He may think, when he casts his vote, it will relate to resumption; but what if gold comes down to par before Congress meets? We thought, when we voted for Lincoln, that the question related to keeping slavery out of the territories; we found out, afterward, that it related to abolishing slavery by civil war in the States.

It is displeasing to our national vanity to find that our government bends less flexibly to the popular will than the English—or, rather, that theirs is perfectly flexible, and ours has no flexibility at all; that they vote on pending and relevant questions; while we vote, at stated times, on past, decided and, now, irrelevant issues.

How did this difference come about? It did not arise because the present English system of flexibility and responsibility was, after due consideration of its merits, rejected by the framers of our government as inferior to that of fixed terms of office. The pages of *The Federalist,* in which Madison, Hamilton and Jay embodied the highest constitutional learning of that day, contain not a single sentence indicating that the element of elasticity existed in the British Constitution, so far as they knew; or that the King was under any constitutional obligation to conform, in his policy, to the views of the House of Commons, by permitting an unpopular ministry to resign, and appointing a new one in harmony with the views of that house. For aught that appears in their writings, the powers of the King were as inflexible—and certainly during the long reign of George III were as inflexibly exercised—as those of the President of the United States, or the Governors of our several States now are. In letter LXIX of *The Federalist,* Alexander Hamilton speaks of the veto power of the King in a manner that no statesman would now employ. He says:

"The King of Great Britain, on his part, has an absolute negative upon the acts of the two houses of Parliament. The disuse of that power for a considerable time past does not affect the reality of its existence, and is to be ascribed wholly to the Crown having found the means of substituting influence for authority, or the art of gaining a majority in one or the other of the two houses, for the necessity of exerting a prerogative, which could seldom be exerted without hazarding some degree of national agitation."

Here, Hamilton ascribes the fact that the Crown had long since ceased to veto bills, not to the fact that the Constitution compelled the Crown to modify its cabinet and its policy to agree with the bill, but to the art with which the Crown succeeded in controlling elections and Parliament. Whether this were true when Hamilton wrote it, or not, it certainly would not be true to-day. To-day, if a bill which the government opposes passes the House of Commons, the cabinet must either resign or dissolve the Parliament, and call an election, in which election the people will decide whether to sustain the old cabinet or the bill. If they elect a new house favorable to the old cabinet, then the bill is dropped. If they elect a new house favorable to the bill, then the old cabinet goes out, and a new one, favorable to the bill, goes in; and hence no bill ever passes both houses, so as to reach the Queen for the royal assent, until her cabinet approve it and are ready to advise her to sign it.

As Blackstone's Commentaries, written a few years earlier than *The Federalist*, nowhere utter this doctrine, that the Crown must modify its cabinet to agree with the House of Commons, though, in practice, it had for some time been the usage, it is probable that it had not then become a doctrine of the English Constitution, but was regarded as most of the features of the English Constitution in their origin were—as a privilege accorded by the favor and grace of the Crown. Certainly there is nothing in the writings of the framers of our Constitution to indicate that they regarded it as a doctrine of English constitutional law at that time.

If we consider the organization of the several colonial governments, we find that this system of ministerial responsibility, not yet fully perfected in England, was not even dreamed of in any of the colonies. They were glad to get representation of the people in a colonial assembly, on any terms, and were not hypercritical as to the delicacy and accuracy of the mechanism by which their representation was had. Short, fixed terms of office were to them a great boon; for what they stood in dread of, was the continuance of the Crown's appointees in office indefinitely, or, perhaps, an imitation, by their colonial legislature, of the long Parliament under Charles I, which would not adjourn at all. The more delicate machinery of a responsible ministry, changeable at the will of the voters, had not then grown into being, and did not occupy their thoughts.

The chief difference between the English government and our own, in respect to the promptness and delicacy with which they respond to the popular will, is one of spontaneous growth, and, so far as all human agency is concerned, of accident. The English never adopted their system as preferable to ours. We never adopted ours as preferable to theirs. Each grew into its own system, without so much as discussing the possibility of the other.

We propose to make a calm and philosophical, but aggressive, comparison between the two, assuming that public opinion in this country, without any reflection, is in favor of our own, and that this *vis inertia*, while it constitutes no argument whatever in behalf of our system, still forms a reason why many will fail to see the wisdom of any reasons that may be adduced in behalf of any other.

And first, in conferring fixed terms of office on our legislative and executive rulers, without the liberty of appealing to the voter at any time to decide whether they shall longer hold office, we have impaired the sense of executive and legislative responsibility to constituencies. Our voting masses can not vote out ministers and overturn majorities in the legislature at the moment when change is needed, viz: when a policy is under discussion and prior to its adoption. We may decline to re-elect the members who have voted for an obnoxious policy, but this not only does not hinder its adoption, but often excludes from the public councils the men who, on the next measure that may arise, would have voted wisely, and in accordance with the public will. Our fixed terms of office, with the barren privilege of punishing a wrong vote by defeat at the next election, to borrow a homely phrase, locks the barn-door after the thief has escaped; while the system of ministerial responsibility, with a privilege of voting against a measure in time to prevent its adoption, locks the thief inside, and takes a vote on the question, "What shall we do with him?"—which is a far nearer approach to popular sovereignty.

It is sometimes assumed that the system of responsibility here would require the office of President be made a life office, or as permanent as the English Crown. This need not be. The Chief Justice of the United States Supreme Court is an officer as permanent, colorless, and free from partisan bias as the Queen of Great Britain. He holds during life, or, what the impeaching powers deem to be good behavior. The Queen hardly does more. The Chief Justice of the highest court of each State may occupy a like position relative to the State government. The Queen's function in dissolving Parliament and calling a new election could be performed by the Chief Justice of the Supreme Court.

The real questions are, whether there is sufficient value in the principle of ministerial and legislative responsibility to pay us for adopting it in our various constitutions, or whether it would work as well here as elsewhere. The chief value of the system is found in the fact that—

1. It admits of a direct vote of the people on all important public measures prior to their adoption.

2. It divides political parties on the living issues actually pending before Parliament, while our system divides them, usually, on dead issues.

And as often as political parties divide on living questions, i. e., on the question what shall actually be done on a matter upon which nothing has yet been done, they necessarily form themselves into a party in favor of the proposed action, and a party in favor of things as they are; in other words, into a progressive and conservative party. Now a division of parties into progressive and conservative, into parties one in favor of action or change and one opposed to change, is philosophical, healthy, and tends toward the permanence and durability of the State   Rome, during the most of its long history, was thus divided into *optimates*, those who believed that things were best let alone, and *populares*, those who believed that popular rights and leveling processes needed perpetual expansion. Great Britain, both at home and in her colonies, from the days of Cromwell to this day, has had these two parties, known, with but little variations, by the same names, viz., Tory or conservative, and Whig or progressive, which is also sometimes styled liberal. Such a division of parties is itself an indication that the people have opportunities of voting on questions of policy. But in our American system, who can tell which party is progressive and which conservative. Those names are never applied to either of our parties, except in a spirit of demagogism, merely to catch votes.. Neither party is at any one time united in favor of action on any one point, or in favor of inaction on any one point. During the agitation of the slavery question, John Brown, who wanted to free the slaves in Virginia by revolution, was a progressive abolitionist, and Senators Toombs and Yancey, who wanted to call the roll of their slaves at Bunker Hill, were progressive pro-slavery men. Lincoln, who was willing to see slavery placed in course of ultimate extinction in the States, but who would grant it every constitutional right even to the fugitive slave law while it lived, was a conservative anti-slavery man, while some of the early generals in our armies who seized rebel cattle but returned to the rebels their slaves, were conservative pro-slavery men.

So. in the questions of protective tariffs, the currency, and finance, of State rights and suffrage, there has at no time been any really conservative nor any progressive party in the country. Whatever action has been taken on these questions has been taken by men elected on other issues. Men elected to prevent slavery getting into the territories have had to decide whether the Union had power to coerce a State. Men elected to maintain the Union by war, have had to decide on the issue of greenbacks and the formation of National banks and granting suffrage to the blacks. Men elected in ratification of universal suffrage, have had to act on civil-service reform. But on neither of these questions have the people had opportunity to vote in advance on what should be done. They could merely vote, inefficiently, after action had been taken.

Now, throughout nature, the machinery which yields most promptly and delicately to its controlling force is the safest. The horse which obeys the rein promptly is safer than one which follows his own bent for a fixed term until he has broken the neck of his rider, and then takes another rider. The revolutions of the heavenly bodies are the least perishable material mechanism in the universe, because every star vibrates responsively to every other, and every orbit is made true by the fact that it is the medium course arrived at by the offset of unnumbered millions of opposing and conflicting attractions, each of which is obeyed in proportion to its weight and in inverse proportion to its distance. Shall it be in government alone that the greatest stability will be reached by giving the people a spasmodic jerk at the wheel on periodical election days, and leaving them at all other and intermediate days with no more voice or control than so many "dumb driven cattle?"

It substitutes in lieu of our present caucus and convention system of nominating the executive in irresponsible party convention, a system of spontaneous and natural selection, whereby the two parties in Congress unite in advancing to the front, as leaders, either of the government or of that opposition which is constantly seeking to supplant the government, the statesmen in whom they place most confidence.

3. The system of responsible ministry imparts more good faith and moral rectitude to politics, in two ways, viz: First, it requires the opposition party not merely to obstruct, but to construct legislation. For it can only oppose a policy on condition, if successful, of taking upon itself to propose and carry out better legislation. Secondly, it compels the people to vote on the direct question before Parliament in this form, viz: Will you vote for Muggins, who, if returned, will vote for Mr. Gladstone's bill to disestablish the Irish church? or, will you vote for Scroggs, who if returned will oppose it? Our issues point back to the previous votes of candidates. The English issue points ahead to his future vote, and its singleness facilitates good faith by compelling the argument to be made on the question actually before the people.

4. It develops in Parliament recognized party leaders, whose ability to maintain their positions in that body depends on their success in satisfying it, from day to day, of the wisdom of their measures. These party leaders are, at the same time, cabinet officers, and thus the executive is brought into closer and more satisfactory relations with the legislature than under our system. The views or intentions of our President and cabinet can be arrived at only by wordy calls for information on the part of Congress, responded to by voluminous and often irrelevant documents. True leadership in Congress and the party will be developed only where cabinet members can be daily cross-examined eye to eye by the opposition. Our institutions fail to develop leaders by any necessity, and if they accidentally arise, fail wholly to place them at the head of the government. Our leadership, if any exists, is the progeny of accident and force. No one would hold Grant to be a political leader in the same sense as Gladstone.

5. It would give the administration the initiative in drawing, framing, and defending before the legislature the proposed law as essential to the success of its work; whereas, under our system, the administration has no constitutional privilege of initiating, drafting or defending the very legislation which it deems indispensable to its success. Judge Story, greatly as he is disposed to laud and magnify the constitution, admits that we have gone too far in separating the executive from the legislative power.

Judge Story (Const. of U. S. Vol. 1, p. 614, § 869) says:

"The universal exclusion of all persons holding office (under the United States, from being members of either house during their continuance in office) is, it must be admitted, attended with some inconveniences. The heads of the departments are, in fact, thus precluded from proposing or vindicating their own measures in the face of the nation in the course of debate, and are compelled to submit them to other men who are either imperfectly acquainted with the measures, or are indifferent to their success or failure. Thus that OPEN AND PUBLIC RESPONSIBILITY FOR MEASURES WHICH PROPERLY BELONGS TO THE EXECUTIVE IN ALL GOVERNMENTS, AND ESPECIALLY IN A REPUBLICAN GOVERNMENT, AS ITS GREATEST SECURITY AND STRENGTH, IS COMPLETELY DONE AWAY. The executive is compelled to resort to secret and unseen influence, to private interviews and private arrangements, to accomplish its own appropriate purposes, instead of proposing and sustaining its own duties and measures by a bold and manly appeal to the nation in the face of its representatives One consequence of this state of things is, that there never can be traced home to the executive any responsibility for the measures which are planned and carried at its suggestion. · Another consequence will be (if it has not yet been,) that measures will be adopted or defeated by private intrigues, political combinations, irresponsible recommendations, and all the blandishments of office, and all the deadening weight of silent patronage. The executive will never be compelled to avow or to support any opinions. It will seem to follow when, in fact, it directs the opinions of Congress. It will assume the air of a dependent instrument, ready to adopt the acts of the legislature, when, in fact, its spirit and its wishes pervade the whole system of legislation. IF CORRUPTION EVER EATS ITS WAY SILENTLY INTO THE VITALS OF THIS REPUBLIC, IT WILL BE BECAUSE THE PEOPLE ARE UNABLE TO BRING RESPONSIBILITY HOME TO THE EXECUTIVE THROUGH HIS CHOSEN MINISTERS. They will be betrayed when their suspicions are most lulled by the executive under the disguise of an obedience to the will of Congress. If it would not have been safe to trust the heads of departments, as representatives, to the choice of the people, as their constituents, it would have been at least some gain to have allowed them a seat like territorial delegates in the House of Representatives, where they might freely debate without a title to vote. In such an event, their influence, whatever it would be, would be seen and felt and understood, and, on that account, would have involved little danger, and more searching jealousy and opposition, whereas it is now secret and silent, and, from that very cause, may become overwhelming.

"One other reason in favor of such a right is, that it would compel the executive to make appointments for the high departments of government, not from personal or party favorites, but from statesmen of high public character, talents, experience and elevated services; from statesmen who had earned public favor and could command public confidence. At present, gross incapacity may be concealed under official forms, and ignorance silently escape by shifting the labors upon more intelligent subordinates in office. THE NATION WOULD BE, ON THE OTHER PLAN, BETTER SERVED; AND THE EXECUTIVE SUSTAINED (or reformed —Ed.) by more masculine eloquence as well as more liberal learning.

"In the British Parliament, no restrictions of the former sort exist, and few of the latter, except such as have been created by statute. * * * The consequence is that the ministers of the Crown assume an open public responsibility; and if the representation of the people in the House of Commons were, as it is under the national government, founded upon an uniform rule by which the people might obtain their full share of the government, it would be impossible for the ministry to exercise a controlling influence or escape (as in America they may) a direct palpable responsibility."

Judge Story does not fully develop the fact that the presence of cabinet members, in the popular branch of the national legislature, is merely an index or incident and not a cause of ministerial responsibility. Its true cause is to be found in the fact that the ministry must resign if they can not commend their policy, either to the house in which it is proposed, or to the house which shall be returned by the people after one dissolution and popular election. Yet, it is clear that the profoundest commentator on the Federal constitution has placed himself on record as the advocate of such modifications as would introduce the element of executive and ministerial responsibility.

6. If the success of the parties were thus made dependent, not as with us, on the aggregated virtue of the party in its handling of all the measures of the previous quarter of a century, mixed and blended as they are at each of our presidential elections into one confused argumentative muddle, but upon the ability of party leaders to justify each measure in a popular election as it arises, a recognized need would be felt for returning the wisest and most experienced statesmen, whether or not they may happen to reside in a district or State favorable to their views or amiable toward their present or past sup-

posed errors. At present, a vote which is unpopular in the representative's district or State "shelves" him forever, without regard to whether he or his successors will vote most satisfactorily on the actual questions on which his successor will be called upon to act. In England, statesmen of the highest ability, when not taken and returned by one district, are by another; the accident of residence being overlooked. Statesmanship is felt to be the essential and all controlling qualification. Our numerous statesmen in private life, and our numerous accidents in public office, sufficiently prove that our constitution does not either develop leaders or insure their hold upon power.

7. The Responsible system would bring to an end the convulsive and increasingly corrupt struggle for the control of the Presidency which now agitates the country to its lowest depths, not only during the year in which the President is elected, but during the years preceding which are spent in plotting for it, and of late, also, during the years following which are devoted to investigating its corruptions and to efforts to overturn its result.

And finally: It is one of the chief and inseparable evils of our system of fixed terms of office and irrelevant political parties that we elect National and State officers, including county and town officers, all on national issues, none of them on State issues. We have no State policies and a very inferior degree of State progress in political matters, compared with what we need and ought to have, and might have if the people were furnished with an opportunity of voting on questions of State policy as they would be if the system of responsible ministry and dissolvable legislatures were adopted in each State.

Suppose at present the real question on which the welfare of Illinois as a State depends, is, by what means can the idle capital, idle labor, idle coal and idle skill of Illinois be combined with the cotton of the south so as to bring the entire cotton crop into this State to be spun and woven, thus increasing tenfold the value of every acre of land in the State, as the building of the Erie canal enriched New York,—we have no machinery by which such a State issue can be brought to the front; but must still keep on "voting as we fought, for the Union." Suppose the first great duty of our State legislature to-day is to furnish us with a speedy, effective system of administering justice, instead of keeping every litigant four years in court, and so virtually denying and abolishing justice,—the utter irrelevancy with which we vote causes us to ask only the candidate's views on the negro and war question, not whether he has given a thought to the duties he is to perform. Now, it is in fact almost as impertinent and irrelevant to ask a candidate for a State office what his views on the national questions are, as to ask an applicant for the position of railroad engineer what are his views on the Trinity.

We now advance to the question, "Would the system of ministerial, executive and legislative responsibility work as beneficially in America as in England?" Are there any circumstances in our "environment" which render ministerial and legislative responsibility impossible? Is our more extended suffrage a reason why we must needs vote in a manner that decides nothing, instead of in a manner that decides everything? In England, household suffrage admits one-fifth of the male adults to vote. In America, manhood suffrage admits them all. If appeals to the country can not as advantageously be taken on actual living questions here as in England, then manhood suffrage is inferior to household suffrage. Conceding this, is it also true that the less the competency of the voter, the greater should be the complication of the issue? Is the voting of the incompetent made safe only when the issues are varied, irrelevant and complex? It is certainly more complex to vote for candidates as Americans do, with reference to the political antecedents of their party for twenty years back, than as Englishmen do, with reference to the single question whether a given thing should be done. It should be born in mind that under the Responsible system, the only issue on which the people can vote will be one on which the administration think one way, and the majority in Congress the other. It surely can not be more dangerous to the public to have the administration act on its views in violation of the will of Congress, or to have Congress act on its views in violation of the will of the administration, as both now do, than to harmonize both branches of the government on one authoritative policy, by calling in the people to decide between them. In so far as universal suffrage lowers the qualifications of the voter, it forms an added reason why he be permitted to vote on a single, unmixed issue. Nor do the extent of our territory, sparseness of our population, and absence of hereditary nobility prevent our adopting the system of ministerial and legislative responsibility; for Canada and Australia have vast territories, sparsely settled, and no titled class worth mentioning, and yet the system works as satisfactorily in both countries as in England. Elections and changes in administration are not, as some would suppose, made more frequent or expensive by the system. Why should the popular will be more fickle or changeable in the United States than in Australia or Canada?

The change would add to the dignity and importance of the office of Chief Justice of the Supreme Court, in case upon this officer should devolve the functions of dissolving Congress and calling elections; and such increase would in like degree lessen and lower the importance of the office of President or Premier. But experience is continually proving that more power and importance centre in the presidential office than any one man is capable of employing for the public welfare, and especially that four-fifths of the 93,000 officeholders now appointed by the President and taught to obey his will, ought to be elected by the people, and taught to obey the law of the land. Why concentrate in an office powers to which no man can do justice?

Let us suppose that all the necessary constitutional amendments have been adopted which would be required to introduce into our Federal government the system of ministerial and legislative responsibility, in lieu of that of fixed terms of office. Members of the House of Representatives are elected, let us say, for a term not to exceed eight years, but liable to be sooner terminated at any moment by the dissolution of Congress by the Chief Justice. The latter, *pro hac vice*, occupies the place of the Crown of England. He is the permanent, colorless and non-partisan element in our constitution. The President may either obtain office on a periodical election, to be held once in say eight years, at which candidates will be nominated by the people at large, or, like the premier and members of the cabinet in England, by first being the leader of the triumphant opposition in Congress. In this case he has been nominated and designated for his position by the opposition in Congress, subsequently ratified by the people of the United States at the polls. To this end, whenever the opposition party in Congress shall propose a vote of want of confidence in the administration in power, they shall accompany it by a list of the names through whom they desire the government to be administered. Upon the occurrence of a majority vote in Congress adverse to the government, accompanied by a list of names of members of the opposition party through whom that party desires the government administered, it shall be the duty of the Chief Justice to order an election throughout the United States, wherein the people will vote for the candidates of the party in power, or for the candidates of the opposition, according to their opinions on the particular policy which gives rise to the question. If Congress should pass a vote of a want of confidence in the existing administration, without being able to agree upon the members of the cabinet desired, then the Chief Justice would select the names from among the leaders of the majority party. The President and his various cabinet members, like the premier under the English system, would continue to be members from some representative district, and to hold their seats in Congress, proposing their policies, introducing their bills, defending them on the floors of Congress, and yielding their executive positions at the head of their respective departments whenever the people should vote a change. It would be essential to such a system that no Representative need reside in the district which elects him, but that all Representatives be chosen from the country at large, though by the people of some one district, and that the patronage of the President be lessened by substituting election for appointment.

Should a candidate running at the same time for Representative of a district and for an executive or cabinet position be elected to the latter, and fail of election to the former, he might occupy the very anomalous position of a member of the cabinet, entitled to a seat in the House of Representatives, but representing no particular district.

Having thus outlined the system, let us suppose it in operation, Mr. Waite being Chief Justice, U. S. Grant, President, and the question before Congress being whether the United States shall redeem its legal tender notes in gold, on demand, on and after the 1st day of January next. If there are 283 members in the House of Representatives, and the administration proposes the measure in question, if 142 members and upward sustain the measure, this continues the existing administration in power, and, their election being the last expression of the popular voice, it is presumed the people are satisfied.

If, on the other hand, 142 votes or upward oppose resumption, the opposition certify to the Speaker of the House, and he transmits to the President, and also to the Chief Justice, a list of anti-resumption candidates for executive and cabinet positions, in manner following, viz:

For President—Thomas A. Hendricks, of Indiana.
For Vice-President—Benjamin F. Butler, of Massachusetts.
For Secretary of the Treasury—William D. Kelley, of Pennsylvania.

For Secretary of State—William Allen, of Ohio.

For Secretary of War—George B. McClellan, of New Jersey.

For Secretary of the Interior—Peter Cooper, of New York.

For Postmaster General—Joseph E. Johnston, of Virginia, etc.

While there need be no constitutional restriction requiring that the candidates so elected by the vote of the opposition members in the House of Representatives should have been the leaders of the opposition in that body, any more than there need be a statute in England enacting that the incoming administration shall be composed chiefly of the leaders of the late opposition, it would, by the force of the interest of the parties, work in that way. This would impart to the debates in Congress a business-like reality and force. That body would no longer be the mere arena for the display of intellectual fireworks, but rather the forge in which, at any moment, a revolution and a new government might be created, and in which the members would speak under the moderating consciousness, not only that their ablest opponents would answer them, but that, if successful, they themselves must take the helm of State, and do something better than that which they are criticising.

The Chief Justice of the Supreme Court, upon receiving the vote by Congress of want of confidence in the administration of President Grant and his cabinet, would issue a writ for an election, in which the people would vote in their respective Congressional districts for such candidates for Congress as they should nominate—those candidates representing, on the one side, resumption, on the other anti-resumption—and also by districts, for the existing executive and cabinet on the one hand, or for the opposition candidates on the other.

Thus it could not fail, that whatever party should elect a majority of members to the House of Representatives, would also elect the President and cabinet, and the complexion and policy of the two would harmonize. The veto power of the President would disappear here, as that of the Crown has done in England, through the complete subordination of that officer to the popular branch of Congress, and the executive and legislative branches would never paralyze action through inability to coalesce in policy. Under our present system, which is an enlargement of the New England "town meeting," first, into a county board of supervisors, then into a State legislature, and then into the National Congress, there is, throughout, no system of selection, except through the party caucus, no recognized party to take the initiative, and no organizing motive to restrain each legislator from defeating the measures proposed by every other, through sheer jealousy. But under the proposed responsible system, the organizing motive, which sorts each party and advances its most powerful leaders to the front, is the instinct or passion for a common success—the same which promotes to the front of a herd of buffaloes the bull of sturdiest courage, broadest shoulders and most invincible horns. It was this instinct to win which compelled George the Third to select Pitt, whom he disliked, and Fox, whom he hated, to lead that administration which, under a sovereign whose name the world has almost forgotten, displayed the greatest executive energy the world has ever seen, in combining the resources of England and the armies of Europe for the overthrow of Napoleon.

The system of "checks and balances," which is supposed by some to have a mysterious value, would disappear, so far as concerns the present power of the President to check and balance anything short of two-thirds of both branches of Congress. The Senate would constitute a check upon the popular branch, but not in so decided a degree as at present; for the very principle of executive and ministerial responsibility, implying, as it does, that the administration shall fight its battle in the popular branch of Congress, would cause the ablest men in the country to seek seats in that branch. There the competitors for cabinet positions and the oratorical thunderers would meet in combats, in which administrations would rise and fall, and revolutions in the personnel of the government would hang on the arbitrament of debate. But by all these means the actual sovereignty of the voting classes over legislative and ministerial action would be made as complete, automatic and sensitive in republican America, as for a century past it has been in monarchical England. Popular suffrage would be less delusive, Presidential elections less dangerous and corrupt, caucuses and National conventions would disappear, and American politics would be less a swindle than they are.

Ten or twelve years ago, in a conversation with Hon. Schuyler Colfax, I ventilated these views in a brief, conversational way, and found that they were familiar guests in his mind. He remarked that he thought the American people might, at an early day, be induced to adopt the system of giving seats in Congress to cabinet·ministers, and that it would work well. About six years ago there were presented in the Illinois legislature a series of resolutions, recommending a re-organization of the National government on this basis. I have not now the resolutions, nor do I remember what action was taken on them, nor the name of their adventurous author.

Last summer I published in the *N. W. Christian Advocate* an article, which is now embodied in this lecture. It was republished, or commented on, in *The Chicago Times* and *Tribune*, *The New York Tribune*, *The Imperialist*, *The Boston Advertiser*, and *The Milwaukee News*, the last named paper being then edited by Hon. John M. Binkley, an experienced Washington politician and editor. *The Chicago Times* characterized the plan above proposed as "a system immeasurably superior to the executive and legislative plan adopted by the twelve colonies." From the remaining critics came either proposed amendments which deny its merits, or humorous fanfaronade, or grave and sombre forebodings at the supposed audacity and impracticability of the scheme. *The Chicago Tribune*, by the pen of its chief editor, Hon. Joseph Medill, suggested that undoubtedly a government, by a responsible cabinet, would be preferable to our present system; but the President ought to remain permanent, as at present, it being sufficient if his cabinet should go out in obedience to the will of the House of Representatives. This is the system over which France has been struggling for nearly ten years, in the effort to discover whether it has a responsible government or not. The value of ministerial responsibility depends on the completeness with which the vote of the popular branch of the parliament changes the government. Under our system, the President, if stubborn, is the government, and his secretaries are his clerks. Mr. Medill's system would effect a change of clerks, and would go far in the right direction. Under a fair-tempered President it might sufficiently change the government. But how could a conscientious President,-elected by one party, work in harmony with a cabinet selected by the adverse party, if the two parties really stood at issue upon living questions? Either their counsels would neutralize and stultify his, (and in that case he might as well have resigned,) or his will override theirs, and in that case they might as well not have gone into the cabinet.

My next critic is *The New York Tribune,* which says:

He advocates a system of legislative and ministerial government in lieu of that of fixed terms of office. He would have members of the House of Representatives elected for a term not to exceed eight years, but liable to be terminated at any moment by a dissolution of Congress by the Chief Justice, who is, he says, "the permanent, colorless and non-partisan element in our constitution." Whenever the opposition in Congress propose a vote of want of confidence in the administration, they shall hand in a list of candidates for President, Vice-President and cabinet officers, and if the motion prevail, the Chief Justice shall order a general election, wherein the people will vote for the administration or the opposition, according to their views respecting the question of public policy on which the division has been made. At the same time Congressmen shall be elected, so that a majority will be in accord with the old administration, if it be retained, or with the new President and cabinet, if they be chosen. The President will be a party leader, the veto power will disappear, cabinet officers will hold seats in Congress, the legislative and executive branches will always be in harmony, the Senate will be a moderate check on the popular branch, and the political parties will be divided on living issues. This is the Professor's scheme. In brief, he would have the nation change, not its clothes, but its very bones. The surgeon who said to a rheumatic patient, "I'll put in a thigh-bone and a shoulder-blade, patch up your spine, work in a full set of ribs, and make a new man of you," was met with the reply, "A post mortem first, doctor."

The fallacy of *The New York Tribune* consists in assuming that the Federal constitution, which is the work of man, is as impossible to mend as the human form divine, which is the work of God. Did not the nation change, not its clothes, but its very bones, when it peacefully and without a tear-drop or a blood-drop passed from the inefficient mis-government of the articles of confederation to the far more efficient system of our Federal constitution? *The New York Tribune* objects to it, because it calls upon the American people for a change utterly beyond our capacity for change.

The Milwaukee News, on the other hand, objects, that while, in the first instance, it would involve a change beyond our capacity for change, in short, a dislocation, in the long run, when adopted, it would call for a degree of stability which we, as a people, do not possess. It says:

CAN WE TRANSPLANT A BRITISH CONSTITUTIONAL DEVICE?

Notwithstanding he chose to publish his views in a journal of limited circulation, in other respects eminently a fit vehicle for the thoughts of serious men—*The Northwestern Christian Advocate*—Prof. Denslow's remarkable paper is having an extensive circulation through the press of the country. We insert it entire elsewhere. If the object of the learned author is to redress the evils under which we suffer with a practical remedy, we think it would be abortive. We see and testify to the symmetry of the theory, and we would especially commend the accuracy and good sense with which he detects and expounds the true nature and working of the English system. But to us it appears that the conditions are so vastly different in America that the introduction of it here would be a violent dislocation.

There is no doubt that the government more directly reflects the will of the people in England than it does in the United States. and this good result is to be imputed to the constitutional instrumentality. But does it follow. that to transplant the instrumentality would command here the same result? We think not. It commands it there only because the conditions temper, favor and regulate it. Those conditions can not be transplanted. We will not enumerate them. But one, alone, will, we think, suffice. British usage is, perhaps, the most impassible, the most invincible, and the most persistent organic system ever known in the world, and it permeates the pettiest trifles of domestic life, as it dominates the most momentous crises of State. We may define any British civil matter whatever, from cab fares to the succession of the Crown, thus: habit, that is—concreted—usage, plus the law. We do not speak of the usage known to lawyers—that is itself law—but usage underlying law, omnipresent, spontaneous, idiosyncratic, English. We can no more transplant that, in transplanting a feature of the British civil constitution, than I can adopt for my own your countenance in adopting your eye-glasses or your cut of beard.

In reply to the metaphysical objections of *The Milwaukee News*, I would say that the English mind is essentially like the American mind. We have a common language, literature, and law, and our American fathers, in laying the foundations of our government, intended to and did adopt every well-matured excellence of the English constitution into our own. But this had not then been well matured. In 1776, it existed only in embryo, and its nature was not even detected then by our astutest statesmen. It has since been matured in England rather by inadvertence than by design. It is the outgrowth of a sense of honor among English statesmen, which forbids them to hold office a moment longer than they represent those whom they serve. In turn, it cultivates the sense of honor of which it is the outgrowth. Does *The News* mean that American politicians have so little sense of honor that no prearranged system can induce them to resign on any contingency? If so, we can take the same course an English parliament would take with an outvoted ministry that refused to resign—impeach them! Does *The News* mean that our national pride would forbid us to borrow this design in politics because it is of English pattern?—we who wear our hair, our whiskers, our overcoats, our boots, our neckties after the English mode, who copy English carriages, carriage dogs, import English blooded-stock, enact English statutes by the thousand, read English literature, and speak the English language; who think an English philosophy, believe in an English phase of religion, and who, it is not to much to say, are Englishmen and worship an English God—we who see our English brethren willing to adopt from us our vote by ballot, our system of recording deeds, our New York code of civil procedure, the principles of which were borrowed from England's illustrious Jeremy Bentham and Lord Brougham, our electric telegraph, our system of propelling vessels by steam, our cylinder printing-presses, our reapers, mowers, sewing machines, and fire engines, willing to receive news through our cable, and to pronounce their own language, under the instruction of the Yankee, Noah Webster? Shall we admit that there is anything the English mind is capable of devising and adopting, that we can not, if we will, put into still more efficient practice than they have done? No. If I may be permitted, for the occasion, to borrow the language of the professional American politician, I would say, I hurl back the imputation with scorn. I believe the two nations will be nearer together in their future competitions, co-operations and destiny than if their governments had never been severed. I would that the north and south were as much in harmony to-day with each other as either the south or the north is with England. I would that more of our railroads pointed toward St. Louis, Memphis and Chicago, and fewer of them toward Liverpool. I would that the domestic commerce, both of products and of ideas, betwe n the various parts of our common country were greater than it is. On its increase depends an increase of the feeling of unity and union. Not less important in producing these results, however, will be such a remodeling of our national constitution as will render it delicately, promptly and justly susceptible to the influences of the popular will, whether the means to that end be of ancient or modern, of American or English, origin Had the system which I have proposed been in vogue in 1858, when a Republi can (John Sherman) was elected speaker of the House, a cabinet would then have come in of Republican views, and rebellion, under such a cabinet, could not have been peacefully matured. It was the long interval under Buchanan's administration, after the republicanization of the north became kuown and before its administration could enter on its duties, that facilitated the peaceful preparation for a vast civil war. It was the sluggish lethargy of our constitution that rendered the rebellion possible, and it yet remains to be seen whether, owing to the same sluggish lethargy, we can ever again suffer a change of parties in our national government without civil war. Certainly the maintenance of the old party in power for six months after it has endured defeat at the polls is not a peaceful nor a prudent feature.

Our constitution was wisely framed for 3,000,000 of people. In many other respects than those to which I have referred, it did not foresee or contemplate the needs of 40.000,000 of people. As after the first revolution it was found necessary that the constitution be wholly remodeled, so after the second revolution, an equally important epoch of constitutional amendment may be at hand. Three most important amendments growing out of the late revolution have already been passed. They protect the negro only. They do not secure purity or ability in the management of public affairs. Our government is more and more becoming the plunder-field of blatant demagogues of both parties, who are too much occupied in serving themselves to ever think of serving the country. Much of this dishonesty in politics arises from the inability of the people, under our system, to vote on living issues. The system of responsible ministry and dissolvable legislatures will not only enable, but compel them to vote on the thing next to be done.

Of course we do not anticipate that such a reform can be adopted in the Federal government before it shall have been adopted in many of the States, as the Federal government will probably always continue to be modeled after those of the States. But once satisfy the American people on a point to which

2

they have hardly allowed themselves to give any reflection, viz., that our system of government is inherently inferior to one that can be substituted, and the subtitution will be easy. The chief obstacle to be overcome is not the national reason, but the national vanity. I regard this quality as a very formidable but not an absolutely unconquerable obstacle. Introduce this system, let the people sway legislation instead of deciding between two sets of officeholders by their votes, and American politics will become more direct, more honest, more able, more efficient, more dignified, and our whole fabric of government will become more stable and enduring because more worthy to endure.

RESPONSIBLE GOVERNMENT.

2. Its Growth, Prevalence and Success as a Principle in Modern Government, Illustrated by Example.

WHILE the advocates of republicanism, both in Europe and America, have been waiting for a century past to see that system supplant the monarchical, there have been silently and gradually developing within the monarchical system certain habits or usages tending greatly in aid of popular freedom, which have come to be known as responsible government. Meanwhile, the attention of the thinkers, statesmen and politicians of our own republic has been occasionally, and of late vigorously, drawn to the fact that it is a government in some respects absolute and irresponsible, our office-holders having a clear *carte-blanche* to do, during their term of office, pretty much as they have a mind, subject only to impeachment for high crimes and misdemeanors.

That republics should grow more absolute, and that the monarchies of Europe should nearly all grow more sensitive to the popular will, is far from fulfilling Napoleon's prediction that in fifty years Europe would become either Cossack or republican.

This subtle change in the constitution of European monarchies so largely satisfies the popular demand, and this unforeseen development of absolutism in republics so disappoints the hopes of republicans, that for twenty-five years past further conversions of European nations to republicanism have been retarded, and instead republicans are inquiring whether the deficiencies in their own system are inherent or accidental.

We purpose to inquire. first, What is responsible government as exhibited in the various national examples in which it has any existence? Secondly, Is the principle indigenous only in monarchies, and an exotic in republics? Thirdly, Can the United States get on well without it? And, fourthly, If not, how shall we introduce it?

NOTE.—The above Chapter 2 was published in the *International Review*, (A. S. Barnes & Co., N. Y.,) for March-April, 1877.

Responsible government is that system wherein the administration is responsible to the Legislature and to the people for every thing that is done, and wherein, to make this responsibility just, the Legislature and people have the means of removing and changing the administration at any moment, to conform to the voice of the nation constitutionally expressed. It implies some one officer sufficiently permanent to act, in great part ministerially, as an appointer of cabinets, a dissolver of Legislatures, and a caller of popular elections, to the end that the executive and legislative branches of the government may, in case of conflict between them, appeal to the voting constituency or people to say which is right; and having so appealed, and the people having voted thereon, their vote shall so control the complexion of the Legislature and of the cabinet that all departments of the government shall bow to the latest expression of the popular will. It is a system under which Legislatures and ministries are dissolvable at any moment instead of being elected or appointed for fixed terms of office, under which the people are appealed to only to decide some living issue on which the Legislature has not yet acted, and under which political parties divide and vote, not with reference to the utility of something already irreparably done, but to the wisdom of something proposed to be done, and on the propriety of doing which the administration in power thinks one way and the majority of the Legislature thinks the other.

This system prevails in the following States in a degree declining in relative vigor or permanency in something like the order in which they are named, viz: the United Kingdom of Great Britain and Ireland, in Canada, in each of the Australian colonies, the Austro-Hungarian Empire, Belgium, Italy, France, the Netherlands, Bavaria, Saxony, Baden and other minor German States, Denmark, Sweden, Servia, Greece, and in the recent constitutions of Spain, Nicaragua and Paraguay. In Switzerland there is a government by a ministry without any executive. The ministry seem to be appointed for short, fixed terms, with certain privileges of rotation, but are without technical responsibility to or power of dissolving the Legislature.

It is absent from Russia, Prussia and the German Empire, most of the minor German States, Turkey,* the United States of America and each of them, Mexico, all the South American Republics 'except Paraguay, Brazil, the Empire of India, China, Persia, Japan, and all barbarous States.

In Great Britain the principle has attained its fullest perfection by growth. In Canada, Australia, and probably Belgium, it has arisen under English influence and imitation. In existing France and Italy it has been adopted through very deliberate preference, and in Austro-Hungary it has been resorted to, by experienced statesmen, to accommodate the interests of a somewhat unpopular reigning family to the persistent demands of the people for the control of the government.

---

* The recent Turkish Constitution provides partially for the substitution of the responsible system of government. The ministry are impeachable by the Chambers, as in Portugal and Brazil, and they have the initiative in framing laws.

In England it seems to have sprung tacitly from the doctrine that the Crown is subordinate to the House of Commons. This doctrine in turn grew out of the exclusive right, so frequently vindicated by the Commons, of originating revenue bills and raising money. Its crowning proofs, however, are to be found in the execution of Charles I, in the supersedure of James II and election of William of Orange, and in the various constitutional laws settling the succession to the crown, and prescribing the qualifications and conditions on which it may be held. The doctrine that the Throne is bound to obey the House of Commons, either as it now is (when a question arises) or as it shall be after one election has tested the popular will on that question, has doubtless been tacitly implied, or at least insisted on, by Whig statesmen since the revolution of 1688. Yet we find George III, in 1782–83, assenting to it so reluctantly, that, rather than retire Lord North's ministry, which had led the war for the subjugation of America, and accept the new Shelburne ministry, in which Pitt and Fox, the champions of American independence, were to be leading spirits, he declared frequently that his honor would compel him to abandon the throne and return to Hanover, and a royal yacht was actually summoned and in waiting to bear him away. Yet in due time he yielded, content to escape the threatened necessity of having Fox himself, whom he chiefly hated, premier. So modern, however, is the blunt statement of this doctrine that the King is subordinate to the Commons, that there is a flavor of radicalism in the exclamation of Mr. Roebuck in 1858: "The Crown, it is the House of Commons!"

The principle undoubtedly has its rise in the power of impeachment, which seems to have inhered in the House of Commons almost as early as any germs of the existence of that House can be traced. Under the Saxon constitution (to 1060) there was no House of Commons. The *Witenagemot* (see Freeman's article in November number, 1876,) included in a crude way the rudiments of a Council of State, a Court of Justice and a House of Lords, but with the informality of a town meeting. It was more like the consultation of an Indian chief with his braves, or of a Czar with the heads of his bureaus. Prof. Freeman's theory, or fancy, that it was a council of all who chose to attend, and that the present House of Lords is the regular successor of the early mass conventions of the common people, irrespective of rank, reduced to paucity of numbers only by the inability and disinclination of the poorer classes to sustain the expense of attending, is barely ingenious. It is at war with the rule that the more barbarous and military the epoch, the more monarchical or aristocratic is usually the organization of society. Local magistrates and county knights may have occasionally sat in the same body as the Lords, but the evidences are, rather, that as early as they sat at all they sat separately as a petitioning body, while the Lords were a legislative body. In 1265, fifty years after Magna Charta, borough representation was first actually witnessed. A century later the House of Commons was strong enough to complain of the King's ministers, and, for the first time, to exercise its power of impeachment. Hallam declares, that at the close of the fourteenth century their consent was necessary to the levy of money taxes, and to the enactment of laws, and that they had frequently exercised the power of inspecting and controlling the administration of government. From this period to the present the King's ministers have been held responsible, in some degree, by the House of Commons, at first rudely, through impeachments and executions, but afterward politely, through resignations; yet, down to the reign of Henry V (1413), the House of Commons, in form, merely petitioned. The King enacted, with the advice and consent of his Lords. An impeachment was in form only the humble petition of the Commons that the King's evil advisers might be arraigned and tried before the Lords.

The responsibility which began as an individual one on the part of each minister, became a collective responsibility on the part of "the ministry" after the revolution of 1688. Thenceforward no ministry waited for the jarring severity of impeachment, but when outvoted besought the Throne to appoint a new ministry, or if the Crown believed the people would sustain the existing ministry, then to dissolve Parliament and order an election. A century earlier Queen Mary had thought it no infraction of the constitution to dissolve several successive Parliaments, with the view of getting one subservient to her wishes. But since the accession of William of Orange, and especially since the failure of the obstinate course of George III towards America, the theory that the King must have no personal policy, but that the House of Commons must fix the policy of the King, has steadily ripened into constitutional law. Sir William Blackstone, writing in the fourteenth to eighteenth years of the reign of George the Third (1774–8), politely and loyally fails to detect the doctrine. Alexander Hamilton, in the sixty-ninth letter in the *Federalist*, impliedly denies any knowledge of the doctrine by asserting that the only reason the King's veto was then in disuse was because the Crown had found it more easy to control Parliament by its arts than by its prerogative   Blackstone may have ignored the doctrine through toryism, and Hamilton may have written sarcastically; but there is more evidence that, in their period, .this was a tenet of Whig politics than that it was an accepted doctrine of the English constitution. History will perhaps award to Queen Victoria's reign the credit of having first displayed the conscientious and admirable non-partisanship, in giving prompt effect to the wishes of either party as it obtained the ascendency in the House of Commons, which was necessary to engraft firmly into the British constitution the principle, so emphatically announced by Roebuck, that the Crown is the House of Commons. This the Queen has done without seeking to influence personally either the popular elections, by which the complexion of the House should be determined, or the course of discussion by which its majorities should be controlled.

The English ministry at present consists of thirty-one persons, of whom from eleven to sixteen form the cabinet, the others being usually heads of bureaus, but not consulting officers of the Crown. The cabinet includes the First Lord of the Treasury, Chancellor of the Exchequer, Lord Chancellor, President of the Council, Lord Privy Seal, Secretaries of State for the Home Department, for Foreign Affairs, for the Colonies, for War, and for India, First Lord of the Admiralty, First Commissioner of Works, Chief Secretary for Ireland, and generally also the President of the Local Government Board, Vice-President of the Education Committee of the Privy Council, and the Chancellor of the Duchy of Lancaster. The selection of the cabinet from among the ministry is not always the same. Generally the Premier has been the First Lord of the Treasury, sometimes the Chancellor of the Exchequer, sometimes both; and sometimes, as in the case of William Pitt, a Secretary of State.

The Crown, through its ministry, takes the initiative usually in legislation, preparing, proposing, and defending in Parliament the bills and measures on which it stakes its success as an administration. So long as these measures are concurred in by the last elected House, they are presumed to accord with the will of the voting constituency. By this very step the administration in power becomes responsible, from the outset, for the measures it introduces, and equally for failing to introduce such measures as it needs for the due operation of the government. There is no shirking the responsibility by saying: "We recommended such a measure, but the House refused to pass it. We piped and ye would not dance." The whole responsibility is thrown on the administration, both with reference to executive and legislative policies, and kept there until it resigns. There can be no deadlock, no checkmate. When the House will not pass the administration's measures, it means that they want a new administration. Parties array themselves, therefore, first in the House of Commons, then at large throughout the country, for or against this living measure. They do not ask whether the ancestors of those who vote with them on this measure, fought for or against their own ancestors, at the Battle of Hastings, or in the Wars of the Roses.

Here begins the contrast with our system in which the administration has no initiative in legislation, except to suggest some measure in a vague way by message, which amounts to nothing until some bill is presented embodying it. When the bill is so presented, it is the work of the member so presenting it only, not of any administration or party. It has no assurance of any support, unless it has previously been agreed on in secret party caucus, and it never can secure a harmonious or majority caucus unless it is germane to, and directly in furtherance of, the one idea on which that party is founded. For instance, the Congressional caucus of a party founded on the anti-slavery idea can never agree on a bill of any kind relating to finance. The caucus of a party formed to vigorously prosecute a war can never agree except on vigorously prosecuting the war. The peace issue of hard and soft money, or protection and free trade, would split it through the middle. The party caucus comes as near as our system admits of to making a party responsible for a bill; but as it only agrees on dead questions, it is worthless as an element of responsibility. It chiefly represents the *vis inertiæ* which causes a party to move on in a given direction, because the track is laid in that line, after the interests of the country require it to advance in some other direction.

The legal status of a member of the British cabinet is that of member of the House of Lords or House of Commons, the latter being the more effective and usual position; and also member of the Queen's Privy Council, a somewhat indefinite body of eminent persons, including many not in the cabinet or ministry. It is as if the President of the United States should, by usage, select his cabinet from among the more prominent members of the Senate and House, these members combining to perform their representative functions in addition to their cabinet duties. The chief legislative duty of an English cabinet officer, after devising measures for the consideration of Parliament, is to defend those measures on the floor of either House. The chief duty of the leaders of the opposition is to carefully avoid opposing a government measure otherwise than by criticism of its details, unless they have something better and more in harmony with the popular will to propose. This induces that habitual moderation, caution and candor which distinguish English speeches in Parliament.

When the wary and prudent leader of the opposition sees his antagonist adopt a policy on which he thinks he can be overthrown, first in the House of Commons, and then, if necessary, before the people, he attacks the offending measure, and the struggle in debate is not for the empty applause of the galleries, but for the control of the government. Each party puts forward its most powerful yet most judicious combatants. It is not a contest of lung power or vituperation, but of pungent wit, of polite humor, of clear statesmanship, of familiarity with the details of government, of dignity of character, of judgment in jurisprudence, of diplomacy and tact. Such a struggle over a critical question sorts men and develops statesmen, by an analysis far finer than any that can be made by our politicians in national conventions, or by any voters at the polls. The younger Pitt and Fox, by the mastery of genius, both led in these debates when they had scarcely passed their majority. But Gladstone and Disraeli were nearly thirty years in Parliament before they attained to the leadership.

The ministry in power, if beaten in such a struggle, may either resign or advise the Queen to dissolve Parliament, and appeal to the voting constituencies. If the latter course is taken, and the voters sustain the existing ministry, it will be indicated by the return of a new House of Commons favorable to the measure which the last one opposed. It will be, therefore, carried, and become a law. The former ministry will remain in power, and the former leaders of the opposition in Parliament, if re-elected to their seats, as they are practically certain to be, will remain leaders of the opposition only. If, however, the voters sustain the Parliamentary opposition, then the new Parliament will be of the same complexion as the previous one, and the defeated ministry, without waiting for impeachment, resign their portfolios. The Queen invites the leader of the opposition to form the cabinet, and he, accepting the Premiership for himself, surrounds himself by advisors of his own party, and the retiring ministers re-enter the House of Commons, of which they have all the time been members, and resume their places as leaders of the opposition to the new administration. It is essential to this system that members of Parliament shall run for any borough or county they please, without regard to residence, as in this way only can the country be sure of returning the statesmen whose services are most needed, by assigning the leaders of each party to boroughs or counties whose political complexion will admit of their election.

This is surely the most admirable system ever devised for sorting and assaying Parliament, for bringing out its fine gold and holding back its dross; for maintaining at all times the ablest advocacy of government measures and the most candid and yet scrutinizing criticism; for maintaining in statesmen complete independence of party or locality, and yet for keeping the administration responsible to and in harmony with the Legislature, and both responsible to and in accord with the people.

The periods during which administrations have held power, have varied from a few months, as under the Duke of Wellington, to sixteen years, as under William Pitt. Parliaments are limited by law to a duration of seven years, and have actually averaged about three and a half. One Parliament may outlast several cabinets, or one cabinet may outlast a series of Parliaments, but every popular election must change the complexion either of a ministry or of Parliament. Thus, the Earl of Liverpool became Premier on June 8, 1812, and continued such until April 11, 1827, holding power nearly fifteen years, surviving the demise of his King, George III, and of four successive Parliaments, and retiring during the pendency of the fifth. On the other hand, the Parliament elected November 4, 1852, saw the Earl of Derby, who was then Premier, succeeded in the following month by the Earl of Aberdeen, and in 1855 by Viscount Palmerston.

Disraeli first rose to the Premiership on February 25, 1868, resigned his power to Gladstone on December 9th following, the people approving of Gladstone's policy of the disestablishment of the English Church in Ireland against Disraeli's opposition. Gladstone continued in the Premiership until February 21, 1874, when he was again succeeded by Disraeli, the elections called pursuant to a dissolution of Parliament in the month previous having resulted in the triumph of Disraeli's conservative policy, the people being opposed to the disestablishment of the Church in England and other kindred policies which were involved in Gladstone's continuance in power.

The average duration of ministries since 1800 has been three years and eight months. In short, while the right of appealing to the people on living issues exists every moment, neither elections nor changes of administration, considered singly, are more frequent than our Presidential contests. Both combined work a change either in the administration or in the Parliamentary majority, at the average, once in twenty months. An election in America is as likely to throw the Executive out of harmony with the Legislature as not, but under the system of responsible government every election restores harmony between the Executive and Legislature, and causes the machinery of government to move on more smoothly.

The revolutions in France for a century past consist of vibrations of the people between Bourbonism, which acknowledges no system of responsibility to the people whatever, either in king or ministry; Bonapartism, which is a modification of Cæsarism or absolutism, acknowledging a certain obligation to popular suffrage, the army and the church, but refusing to make this obligation tangible by allowing the ministry to be held responsible to the Chamber of Deputies; Orleanism, under Louis Philippe and his Minister, Guizot, which adopted and attempted to maintain the system of responsible ministry and dissolvable legislatures, substantially as in England; and republicanism, which in its earlier experiments relied only on short terms of office and impeachment as a means of holding rulers responsible, but which in its last experiment, the existing republic, has established for our example a more permanent executive, a ministry responsible to the Chamber of Deputies, and a dissolvable Chamber. By the constitution of February 25, 1875, the President is elected, for a term of seven years, by a majority of the votes of the Senate and Chamber of Deputies united in National Assembly. He is removable only on impeachment for high treason, but every official act or order on his part must be countersigned by a minister. Each minister is responsible individually for his personal acts to the Chambers, and "The Ministry" as a body is responsible for its measures, which responsibility it accepts by resigning when outvoted in the Chambers unless the President, with the assent of the Senate, shall dissolve the Chamber, in which event an election must follow within three months. It would seem, therefore, that the President and Senate combined might continue an unpopular ministry in power, and this may prove an imperfection in the working of the French system. The President is re-eligible, and has command of the army and the usual incidents of executive power. The Senate is composed of 225 Senators, elected for nine years, by the departments of France and the Colonies, and 75 life-members, first nominated in the joint session of the Senate and Chamber of Deputies, known as the National Assembly, and afterward elected by the Chamber of Deputies alone. The Chamber consists of one deputy for each *arrondissement*, and of one for every 100,000 population which any *arrondissement* may contain in excess of the first. The present assembly was elected in 1871. The system has not yet been tested by a popular election, but, judging from its workings thus far, it is better adapted than any hitherto known to France to secure sensitiveness to the will of the people, and to develop powerful parliamentary statesmen.

The Austro-Hungarian Empire, under the Constitution of 1867, presents apparently one of the most complicated and yet skillful combinations, extant, of local self-government, or state's rights and federative union, with government by responsible ministers and dissolvable legislatures. Except the Emperor, no official has a certain term of office. The empire is dual in form, embracing the two independent kingdoms of Austria and Hungary, which are united in their sovereign, their army, a part of their treasury, and their foreign affairs, but each of which has its own legislature and its own responsible ministry in all other matters. The Legislature of Austria proper is federal, consisting, in its Upper House, of nobles, archbishops, and life-members nominated by the Emperor, and, in its Lower House, of 353 delegates, nominated by the Provincial Diets (state legislatures) of 17 provinces, and elected by the direct vote of all citizens possessing a very small property qualification.

The Reichstag of Hungary, on the other hand, is itself a local legislature, though it admits into its Upper House 5 magnates in all, and in its Lower House 110 delegates, from Croatia, Slavonia, and Transylvania.

The Hungarian and Austrian legislatures unite in choosing "the Delegations," which are a joint Imperial Congress of 120 members, for passing on questions common to the entire kingdom; whose membership is very simply composed of sixty members, chosen by each legislature, twenty by its Upper and forty by its Lower House. Thus Austria has three grades of federally united legislatures—namely, the Imperial, Austrian, and Provincial. Huugary has two, the Imperial and Hungarian. Three of the Emperor's ministers—namely, his Minister of Foreign Affairs for the whole Empire, his Minister of War for the whole Empire, and his Minister of Finance for the whole Empire—are responsible to the Delegations. Besides, there is a ministry in eight departments for Austria responsible to the Austrian Legislature—namely, the Presidency of the Council. and Ministries of the Interior, of Finance, of Education and Religion, of Agriculture, of Commerce, of National Defense, and of Justice.

A similar ministry of nine persons, including a minister near the King's person, *ad latus*, is responsible to the Hungarian Legislature. The sovereign is King of Hungary, Emperor of Austria, aud in acts common to the whole empire is styled Emperor of Austria-Hungary. The seventeen Provincial Diets of Austria are without local cabinets, their executive officers being either appointed by the Crown or elected by the people and approved by the Crown. This admirable compromise, by which complete autonomy is granted to Hungary without lessening the dignity of the Empire, is mainly resultant from the statesmanship of Von Beust applied to reconcile the unconquerable resistance of the Magyar race to Austrian subjugation, and the equally persistent determination of the House of Hapsburg not to abandon its Hungarian kingdom. What the Hungarians failed to secure by their gallant revolution under Kossuth, in 1848, they fully secured by passive refusal to send representatives to an Austrian Legislature. The history and success of this example of passive resistauce would form an exceedingly interesting lesson to all revolutionists, indicating, as it does, that peaceful methods may often be found effective, where warlike methods fail, to disinthrall a subjugated and conquered people.

In the states composing the present German Empire, the principle of responsible ministry is avowed by Bavaria, Saxony, Baden, Oldeuburg, Brunswick, Saxe-Weimar and Saxe-Meiningen, while it is rejected by most or all of the other states, by Prussia, and by the Imperial Government itself. The Imperial Legislature consists of an Upper House (Bundesrath) of 59 members, elected by the states, of whom Prussia has 17, and a Lower House (Reichstag), 397 in number, chosen by universal suffrage, Prussia electing 236.. The ministry of the empire consists of a Chancellor (Von Bismarck), who is responsible only to the Emperor, who in turn rules by divine right, and is responsible only to God. The struggle in Prussia on the organization of the army, in the years 1858 to 1864, was practically a struggle of the legislature for responsible government—that is, for the power to control the Crown by refusing to vote supplies; but the King first proved his power to go on and maintain the army at his own standard by the aid of the army itself, without a legislative vote of supplies, and then during a succession of vigorous wars, redounding greatly to the glory of the German name, vindicated the military sagacity of the course he had pursued in abridging the liberties of the people.

The German people are now in fact being schooled in the art of government and educated in its forms, without being all at once intrusted with its real power. A deep reverence for scholarship, and especially for learning in jurisprudence, is manifested wherever the German race bears sway. Learned doctors of the law who have been graduates, and some of them instructors in the universities, and who have given their lives to the study of jurisprudence, are accorded a position in practical legislation and administration side by side with successful generals and noblemen, a position which in America is only to be won by a happy faculty of telling anecdotes on the "stump," or by expending several thousands of dollars in buying a political convention.

In Russia, where there is no elected parliament whatever, but the entire administration is carried on by bureaus, responsible to the Emperor alone, there is not yet laid even the foundation on which responsible government could be based. In Switzerland there is a system of government by a some, what flexible and rotating ministry without any other executive than the head of the ministry; but there is no dissolvable legislature, and therefore no other responsibility than results from short terms of office. In Brazil, representation in one Imperial legislature, federally united with many provincial legislatures has been introduced, but the machinery of government is by far too autocratic to admit of responsibility to the legislature being yet accepted by the Emperor or his ministry, except that the latter can not plead the Emperor's orders in defense or extenuation if they violate the law.

In at least one colony of Australia (West Australia), during the year 1875, the attention of the people was so directly called to the subject of responsible government as to result in its being substituted for the system of fixed terms of office which they had previously tried.

We have thus cursorily opened up rather than answered our first question, namely, What is responsible government as exhibited in the various national examples now extant? To answer it fully by tracing the workings and results of the system in each would expand this brief article into a political library. In all these governments it operates alike to bring on elections only when the decision of the people is needed on some great issue or policy; to allow no such issue to be decided or acted upon without an appeal to the people; to divide parties only on living issues, thus constantly burying dead prejudices; to educate office-holders into a high and honorable sense of their accountability to the people; to make statesmanship a permanent pursuit followed by a skilled class of men, not a political accident availed of by charlatans and adventurers; in short, to render politics honest and respectable.

Our second inquiry is, whether responsible government is indigenous only in monarchies, and an exotic among republics; in short, does it require a king? Many republics, doubtless, have existed without it. The nearest approach Rome ever made to the principle of responsibility to the people was very unlike in method, and consisted in the theory that no law (*lex*) could be adopted without the consent of the entire people voting in *Comitia*. Among modern republics only France has adopted it, unless we recognize the somewhat dubious experiments in Nicaragua and Paraguay. All these are chiefly significant as showing that of late no new republics are started on our system. Even the recently "convict" settlements of England in Australia, one and all, discard fixed terms and demand responsibility. Much of the absence of this principle from the Mexican and South American republics is due to its absence, in 1780, from the United States. It was absent here because it was not then well matured in England; because our statesmen, as their writings show, were wholly unfamiliar with it; because our colonial governors had no ministers; and because the colonists thought short, fixed terms of office were the very best means of holding officers to account, in which impression they were evidently in error. A comparison of these data shows that this principle has developed more frequently in connection with a permanent executive. But as this is largely owing to our own example, a reversal of our example would probably, in due time, reverse the argument.

Our third question is, Can the United States get on well or at all without this system of responsibility? It involves an inquiry into the evils incident to fixed terms of office.

The chief glory of republics is, not that they promise the most trained capacity in the administration of affairs; for this they have seldom been supposed by any class of statesmen or publicists to do; not that they promote the highest degree of order; for they are certainly more anarchical than other forms of government; but that they are supposed to represent most faithfully the interests and will of the people. If, therefore, with less of wisdom and of order, they combine less fidelity to popular interests, their cause is lost. It is an axiom in human nature that agents who can not be held to account can not be held to fidelity. There never was an exception to the rule, and can never be. Suppose a principal in New York to have a property in Chicago which he is unavoidably compelled to depute an agent to manage for him. Suppose an individual capable of being so absurd as to agree to appoint an agent for a fixed term, say four years, with no other power of calling him to account in the mean time than either to impeach him for crime or to remove him and appoint another agent, also for a like fixed term. Who does not see that under such a system the most honest agents would be turned into swindlers? Suppose, on the other hand, he should depute two men, each to watch the other and report. Each should be agent until the other could prove him at fault; then the other should take his place until proved guilty of like fault. The estate would be as well managed as if it were under the direct charge of the principal.

Our so-called republican system is that of change of agents at the end of fixed terms. It is incurably bad, because it does not make honesty promote a politician's personal interest so much as dishonesty. An irresponsible trustee for a fixed term has the largest possible interest in robbing the trust fund. A system of government which, to work successfully, demands that men shall be self-sacrificing, or that human nature should be abolished, is a failure from the start. The responsible system says to every office-holder, " Ye know not the day nor the hour." Therefore he must be always ready to render his account. No pains on the part of the people, in nominating or electing officers, can counteract the incurable evils of a system which inherently tends to promote incompetency and knavery.

For instance, in 1858 the House of Representatives became Republican, but by our system of fixed terms the President could neither be changed nor checkmated until 1860. The intermediate two years witnessed the anomalous spectacle of the officers in charge of a government conspiring for its overthrow, distributing its army throughout the South and discharging it, with the expectation that its officers, rank and file, would enlist in the Southern service, and sending its arms and munitions of war where enemies could best capture them. Had the principle of responsibility existed, Buchanan would have had to appoint a Republican cabinet, consisting of men like Seward, Lincoln, Chase, and Sumner, in 1858, and the Civil War would perhaps have been impossible.

But as our elections are held solely because we have reached the period for holding them, not because there is any issue to be voted on; as our mixed and muddled issues under the system of fixed terms relate to the past only, not to the future; as voting on past issues is totally frivolous at the best, many of our voters, as if to make them as frivolous as possible, vote as far back in the past as is necessary to gratify their innermost spite. Put up an Orangeman in a Catholic district, and lo! the issues relate to Cromwell's invasion of Ireland, two centuries ago. Put up the grandson of a Federalist, and the issue is the War of 1812. From 1840 to 1860 all Irishmen voted the Democratic ticket, though it meant the extension of slavery, because, forty years earlier, Democratic leaders had given the ballot to the Irishmen. After President Jackson had crushed the National Bank, the people voted on its propriety. After Polk had made war on Mexico, the people voted on whether he ought to have done so. After Texas was annexed, the people voted on that. And after the compromises of 1851 concerning slavery, the people kept on voting as to whether those compromises were right or not, until the breach widened into war. Had we been under responsible government, the people would have voted on the compromise *before* it was adopted; and that, and that alone, can make any legislation a finality. Officers elected in the South on the platform of extending slavery into the territories, and in the North on that of keeping it out, decided, without consulting the people on either side, that the South would rebel, and that the North would subdue the rebellion. In 1864–65 the Republican party, elected on the issue of vigorously prosecuting the war, enfranchised the negro, of course without consulting the people. Having done so, certain congresses, elected on the crab principle to ratify these things already done, proceeded without consulting the people, to contract the currency. Thus, under our system of fixed terms, the issues pending when legislatures are elected are seldom those on which they are to act, but generally those on which they have already acted. Hence, while the people are voting when it is too late, legislators are without instructions and without any authoritative mode of getting them. This causes legislation to drift without a helm, over the wide waste of individual speculation and aimless, disorganized, nomadic effort. For fifteen years past Congress has had no financial policy whatever, and has been incapable of maturing one, solely from this inherent defect in its organization. Each bill that any one member introduces is assailed by every other through jealousy, lest some one member may get the credit of affording financial relief to the country. In such an event every other member, under our system, sees only detriment to himself, whereas, under the "responsible" system, the measure introduced by the administration would first be devised by the wisdom of the entire cabinet, which would give it a prestige and probability of wisdom which no measure devised by a single member could have; it will then be criticised by the opposition, but not opposed unless the opposition are ready to name a definite policy against it and make it a test question. Thus, under the responsible system the opposition are driven to unite upon a policy or measure, as well as the administration. There can be no irresponsible guerilla warfare pursued against a measure. All measures are in effect either those of the administration or the opposition, and each member finds it to his interest to support either the one or the other. This avoids paralysis of legislation, a result which is of infinite value in that very large class of questions of business and finance, in which the adoption of either one of twenty proposed plans is better than the failure to adopt any.

In no work on political science, which has yet come under my notice, is this effect of fixed terms of office, in both executive officers and legislatures, to cause paralysis of legislation, or even to cause the people to vote on dead issues, pointed out. It is not remarkable, therefore, that neither legislators nor people have given it their reflection. When they do, they can not fail to admit that the system renders our elections vapid and meaningless, dishonest and irrelevant.

"Does the pending question before Congress relate to the currency? Then vote for Jones, because he is sound on the negro and on the war." Why rebuke respectable voters for despising the polls? It is the man who votes under such a system that is the fool. Pulpits filled by preachers who never vote, wax eloquent in rebuking pews filled with merchants that never vote. The conduct of both is sounder than their theory. When voting can do no good, it is the part of men of sense to cease voting; and voting to indorse this or that political party, by electing its candidates, does no good.

Nothing can be more conducive to universal dishonesty and fraud in politics, than to call on the people periodically to vote on that inextricable muddle of shams, prejudices and impositions, that perfectly irrelevant proposition, "the record of a political party."

But while in any state of the country it converts popular elections into a farce, in some exigencies it renders them only less disastrous, in themselves, than a financial crisis or a war. The entire campaign of 1876, however it may result, has been an unmitigated curse to the country. When it began, the country was at peace, and, had we been under a responsible government, no issue could have been made up for the people to vote upon, except one on which the Administration had taken one side and the House of Representatives the other, and it must have related to the immediate business before Congress, which was then the question of expansion of the currency. A canvass on such a question, could it have been had, would have obliterated color lines, rebel lines, loyal lines, and all other lines connected with slavery, the negro, and the war, and would have been infinitely serviceable and instructive to the country. But under our crab system of going forward by looking backward, the only question possible was the utterly pernicious, useless and infernal one, "Will you vote to indorse the past record of the Democratic Party or of the Republican Party?" or, as it soon came to be put, "Will you vote for the Union or for the Rebellion of fifteen years ago?" This re-opened all the issues of the war, brought our submerged hell up again to the surface, and sent it round belching blood and brimstone through the land. Can a system be more fatal to liberty than one which renders a popular election a national calamity, which, instead of instructing administrations, revives civil war?

All these evils are inherent, not in republicanism, but in irresponsibility —in fixed terms of office. Give England the system of fixed official terms and stated periodical elections, and her elections will soon be as meaningless and her officials as contemptible as ours. Her statesmanship will fade into a mere memory, as ours has done, and fraud and force will run the empire. Must we be borne along as was France under the irresponsible absolutism of Napoleon III, until we, like the French, are paying taxes for a paper army of 1,400,000 men, of whom 1,100,000 do not exist? Manufacturing munitions of war, and packing them away so scientifically that, before they could be unpacked and put together for use, the enemy were crowning their king emperor in the French capital? Must we, like France, cross over the deep and dark chasm of communism before we can pass from the irresponsible absolutism of our petty emperors of an hour, our horde of governing pismires, to a system of dignity, responsibility and good faith? We have seen the generous purse of the nation transferred to credit mobiliers, syndicates, and gold brokers. We have seen the sovereignty of the people, the power to elect to office, transferred from the people to a returning board. It is but a short step from a returning board, authorized to elect whom it may prefer, to an emperor, authorized to dispense with elections altogether.

I would not attempt to predict, whether through calm discussion or through national disaster and revolution, the American people will be driven to adopt responsible government. But if, as I believe, all responsible government is subversive of liberty and of statesmanship, and unfit for a free people, then will every instinct of the American people drive them ultimately to exchange the irresponsible for the responsible form. As it is, in no country do the people feel such an overwhelming sense of the littleness of the men in charge of public affairs. In no country are the officials so conscious that they are contemptible. In no country is there a national legislature and cabinet so rapidly retrograding, so certainly sinking into the hands of men ignorant alike of letters, law, history, finance, and even of the morals and manners of gentlemen.

Having sufficiently noticed the evils of our system, we now advance to our fourth inquiry—namely, how shall we set about introducing a better?

All, we believe, that is needed to bring the people to adopt responsible government is to bring them to understand it. It is more in harmony with the instincts of all honest men than the system of fixed terms of office. If the peasantry of Austria, France, Hungary, Norway, Sweden and numerous German

States, and the ex-convicts of Australia can vote under it, it surely will not be said that it requires too much intelligence for the average American voter!

If responsible government simplifies the issue by reducing the question to the one issue—as, for instance, shall we resume? shall we expand? shall we have war? etc.—it is certainly as easy (in addition to being far more effective) for the people to vote intelligently on this issue in advance, as it is to have an uninstructed legislature and executive act on it; and then to be called on afterward to vote for a set of candidates of both parties, each of which had some members who voted one way and some who voted the other, and each of which is ready to claim to a voter who is ready to indorse a given course of action that it is the responsible author thereof, and to a voter who opposes that course that it is in no degree responsible for it. Thus, in our recent campaigns both parties have been for "resumption" in New York and for "expansion" in Indiana; for "free trade" in Illinois, and for "protection" in Pennsylvania. Surely voters who are competent to find out the wiser course amidst so much duplicity would have even less difficulty if the issue were one, and that a straightforward one, than if, as now, the issues are many and complicated.

Two methods of accomplishing responsible government in the United States have been proposed, one of which is supported by the Chicago *Tribune* and the other by the Chicago *Times*. Should an equally full discussion elsewhere provoke an equally harmonious support of the general principle, the question would be resolved into one merely of details. The first is after the existing French model, namely, that the President and Congress be elected for a somewhat permanent term, say of seven years, and that his cabinet only be responsible to Congress in the technical sense, he being only removable by impeachment and conviction for crime. This might be expressed in an amendment to the constitution, somewhat as follows:

The executive power of the United States shall be vested in a President, to be chosen for a term of seven years by the people (or by Congress, as might be preferred), the members of whose cabinet shall form a ministry, responsible to the House of Representatives, collectively, for the general conduct of the government, and individually for the acts of each member. The President may be removed only on impeachment for and conviction of crime. Each executive act, to be valid, shall be countersigned by the minister of the department to which it relates. Ministers shall be collectively and individually removed on impeachment by the House alone, without trial, for conduct disapproved by the House.

The legislative power shall be vested in the President and ministry, and in a Senate and House of Representatives to be constituted as heretofore, except that the Representatives shall be elected for seven years, subject to the earlier termination of their office by the causes herein provided. The President shall select his ministers from among the members of either the Senate or the House, and shall, through his ministry, have the initiative in legislation in common with members of either house, and the right of debate on all matters pending therein.

Whenever a majority of the House shall oppose any measure introduced or sustained by the administration, the President shall either remove from his cabinet the members responsible for such measure, or, if he believes that such members, and not the House, truly reflect the will of the people thereon, he shall, with the consent of the Senate, dissolve said House, thereupon immediately ordering a new election of Representatives to be held within thirty days

—3

after such adverse vote—such Representatives to continue in office for seven years from the period of such election, or, until the next dissolution of Congress.

It shall not be necessary for any Senator or Representative to reside in the State or district which he may be chosen to represent, or to resign his seat if, after being so chosen, he shall be appointed to a cabinet office; but no Senator holding a cabinet office shall draw any other pay than that pretaining to his position in the cabinet.

This renders the President permanent, except in case of impeachment for crime; but he is shorn of his power, except as he may exert it through a responsible minister, *i. e.*, one removable at the will of the House. The other method would resemble the government of Switzerland in the fact that the executive powers would be vested in a ministry, and not in one person; but would differ in the fact that the ministry would have the power of dissolving the legislature, and would be responsible to the legislature, as in England, instead of being, as in Switzerland, elected for fixed terms.

The entire ministry would retire together at the will of the House, or appeal to the people. It is advocated by the Chicago *Times*, and might be expressed in a constitutional amendment like the following:

The executive power of the United States shall be vested in a responsible Ministry of eight persons, the chief officer of whom shall be called the President of the Ministry. The Ministry shall be elected by the Congress (or by people, as may be deemed desirable) by a ballot which shall designate the position to be occupied by each person voted for, simultaneously with the election of the first Congress to be chosen under this amendment, and shall hold for seven years, unless sooner dissolved, impeached or resigned. The Ministry shall be members of either House *ex officio*, but may not vote. Upon a vote in the House of Representatives, adverse to any measure or course of said Ministry, accompanied by an agreed list of candidates to succeed said Ministry, the said Ministry shall stand removed unless the President of the Ministry, with the consent of the Senate, shall dissolve said House, and appeal to the country by ordering an election of Representatives to be held within thirty days after such dissolution.

The legislative power shall be vested in a responsible ministry, permanant Senate, and dissolvable House of Representatives. The members of the latter shall be elected each for the term of seven years, subject to the earlier dissolution of the House by the Ministry.

No Senator or Representative need reside in the State or district for which he may be chosen, but any Senator or Representative, accepting a cabinet position, shall receive only the pay of the latter.

Both these provisions agree in opening up the Senate and House to the freest competitions between the best minds in all parts of the country. The theory that each county seat shall produce its local statesmen, and that no Congressional district shall have any higher order of calibre than it may happen to produce, is as preposterous as that each county shall have no sugar, cloth or iron that it does not produce. It fosters local and sectional narrowness, meanness and hatred, and prevents statesmanship from becoming a permanent profession to any man, however worthy.

Still another mode, which has already been widely published, is to have the Chief Justice of our Supreme Court perform the strictly ministerial functions, which in England are performed by the Queen, or in France by the President, in dissolving legislatures and calling elections. These are questions of detail and belong to the future.

The language in which a law is couched is but its husk. The kernel must be found in its spirit and genius. If these are laid upon deep and immutable principles of human nature, and especially if their wisdom is fortified by illustrious historic examples and by long traditions, it is not innovation but conservatism to adopt them. If they have hitherto, wherever tried, resolved chaos into order, libertinism into liberty, and passion into law; if they have substituted statesmanship for standing armies, and jurisprudence for demagoguery, then they are planned well. That these would be the tendencies of responsible government in America we expect to see Americans generally, at an early day, come to admit. When they do, its adoption will quickly follow, and our republic will have entered on its second epoch. Its first revolution relieved it from the mastery of a foreign State; its second revolution would lift it into the command of its own tendencies to anarchy and misrule, and make it master over itself.

Among many utterances of the press, in response to the above article, we select the following from the *Boston Advertiser:*

RESPONSIBLE GOVERNMENT.

The International Review has an article by Professor V. B. Denslow upon the above subject, which is one among many significant signs of the times. All great changes in the world's history have been merely the concrete result of long previous preparation. The state of the Roman empire seems to have been expressly adapted to the coming of Christ. Luther, it has been often remarked, was merely the one man to give voice to the feeling of his time. Even the application of steam and electricity came upon a world demanding and all ready to receive it. And the people of the United States, wearied with the unmeaning jingle of parties, disgusted with the inefficiency of government and the want of correspondence between the interests of the country, and of the men who assume to control it, appear to be pretty nearly ripe for the introduction of a new principle. Responsible government can be easily shown to be an indispensable necessity for the ultimate success of free institutions, and has been adopted in other countries in proportion as the people have been admitted to a voice in their public affairs. Yet there is hardly a trace of it in the government of the United States as a whole or the individual parts. If the readers of these columns need any further illustration of the absurdities of our methods of conducting public affairs, they are referred to Professor Denslow's article. But the trouble with the increasing number of those whose ideas of remedy are taking the same direction is, that they ask too much. If they can not have Abana and Pharpar they will have nothing to do with the waters of Israel. Thus Professor Denslow holds a dissolvable legislature, actual membership of the House on the part of cabinet officers, the removal of all restrictions upon residence, and united ministerial responsibility, to be essential, while others connect with these things longer terms of the executive or legislature, or both, the cabalistic period of seven years being supposed to have great virtue. But any such changes require constitutional amendments, which for three principal reasons are simply impossible. First, they involve an entire reconstruction of the framework of our government, and of the difficulties of this, at the present day, the reader of Elliot's debates can form a faint idea. Second, such amendments must pass, not only Congress, but twenty-seven legislatures, and, as in increasing the responsibility, they must perforce increase the independent power of the executive and diminish that of the legislatures and of the politicians composing or ruling them, the absolute and uncompromising hostility of the latter to the very principle is the one element that can be counted on with certainty. Third, it is impossible *a priori* to devise a new system which shall cover all requirements and be so evidently desirable as to excite the requisite popular enthusiasm. Before we can overcome these obstacles the chances are much greater that we shall go to pieces in anarchy and reunite under a military despotism. We might as well try to establish a House of Lords at once.

Taking things as they are, then what is there that is *practicable?* Let us consider the situation of the incoming administration. It is such that the most ardent Republican must have a half wish that the burden had been thrown upon Mr. Tilden. There will be a Democratic majority in the House. Small, perhaps, in number, but smarting under disappointment and defeat. The majority of the Senate is nominally Republican, but, apart from the chances of an early change, it is in the hands of men wedded to all the abuses of the past. Unless the President plays into their hands, their hostility will be just as great, and none the less deadly for being secret. If he fails to appoint a cabinet of honest and independent men, he will lose the country and seal the fate of the Republican party. If he does appoint such, the knife will be put to his and their throats by those who should be his party friends. Not giving office to Democrats will excite hostility in the House, but little greater than failure to satisfy party claims will excite in the Senate. Investigating committees of the House will discover what they desire, and nothing more, and half-hearted support in the Senate with lead the country to believe that their reports are true. Persecution will force its way into every corner of the White House and the departments. What is the natural refuge of honest officials in such straits? Appeal to the country. But from this they are entirely cut off. The public never can or will know the story of their wrongs. But suppose President Hayes to say to Congress: "Neither I nor my officers shrink from any examination, provided it is public, and where both sides can be heard. Instead of calling the latter at your pleasure into committee rooms, where their evidence can be garbled, admit them to the sessions of the House. Let question and answer be individual and public, and let the country judge." If we can not have a responsible ministry start forth fully armed, like Minerva from the head of Jove, we can at least take the first step, and leave the rest to time. The cabinet need not at once take the guidance of legislation. They do not have it now, and they need not then. They would stand against an adverse majority. but they will occupy that position at any rate. The opposition would be public and not secret, and they would have protection from their friends, which they will need a great deal more than from their enemies. Assuming them to act at first merely as witnesses, we might get no great gain in legislation, but we should get what is of more immediate importance,—a greater degree of purity. If a cabinet officer were pressed by either side to do what was against his conscience, a visit to one or two members on the other would elicit questions which would soon free him from such importunity; while. if he were tempted to yield to such pressure, the least suspicion on the other side would at once bring the whole matter to light. For the very reason, however, that such a step would arm an independent President against both sides, both sides will agree in refusing to take it. It must be forced upon Congress. But a suggestion by the President in his message, with a few hints dropped to the newspaper reporters, would rouse public opinion to a point which our legislators would hardly venture to resist.

We will add only one reflection: The Republican party has one more chance. If things go on in the old way, and they must under the present system, the President will go out with damaged reputation, and the party will disappear forever. Four years will have been lost, and it will take at least four years more to convince the country that the Democrats in power will only make matters worse. The country will be very lenient in the matter of achievement, if it can be fully satisfied as to the purity of administration. If the sincere Republicans and the President have any regard for their future they will see to it that that purity is attained and demonstrated in the only way in which it can be,—by public executive responsibility.

TAXATION AND REPRESENTATION;

OR,

THE RIGHTS OF CAPITAL IN GOVERNMENT.

———

THE United States of America became a nation in vindication of the principle that taxation and representation are inseparable, *i. e.*, that only those who pay the taxes should have the power to impose them. This is an English principle, and grew up out of the theory that the Crown was self-supporting out of its own private lands and revenues, as originally it was, and only needed the aid of taxes, or as they were called in England extraordinary revenues, to help it out in emergencies. Great Britain fought to subdue the thirteen colonies, in the groping after another principle, not then very clearly understood, viz: that expenditure and taxation are inseparable. The mother country had expended several millions during the wars known here as the Queen Anne's and French and Indian Wars, in sending over regulars under Braddock and Montgomery to defend the colonies from the French and Indians, and in part with an ultimate view to capture the Canadas from the French. These expenses caused an illogical void in the British budget. Why should the people of London or Yorkshire, Scotland or Ireland, India or Australia be taxed to defend the American colonies from their French and Indian neighbors, or to conquer the Canadas for the future security of the thirteen colonies? Yet the tax to reimburse the treasury had to be drawn from somebody somewhere. What policy more logical or just than to draw it from the people who had asked for and been specially benefited by the expenditure? But "no" said Massachusetts, New York and Virginia, " we will not pay the tax, though we concede that the expenditure benefited us especially, because government ceases to be constitutional and free when taxes can be imposed by any others than those who pay them." Out of this principle our nation was born.

It is the purpose of this lecture to show, first that the American people failed to put into absolute practice the theory they then fought to inculcate into the British mind; thus illustrating Shakspeare's witticism:

> "'Twere easier to teach twenty what 'twere well to do,
> Than be one of the twenty to follow our own teaching."

And secondly, that we would be greatly benefited as a nation by giving to this principle its full scope and effect.

England has maintained in her other colonies the theory for which she then fought, that expenditure and taxation are inseparable, that the expenses of India shall be paid by taxation upon the Hindoos, those of Canada by Canadian taxes, and those of Australia by taxes on the Australians.

The American States, on the ratification of their independence, attained to full power to apply the principle, that taxation and representation are inseparable, and supposed they were applying it when they provided in the various State constitutions that all adult male citizens should vote, that there should be a representative to a certain quota of population, and that all property should be taxed according to its value. It was scarcely observed, so equal was then the diffusion of property, that many would vote who paid no taxes, and that many who paid taxes would have no vote, and that, in short, they had divorced representation from taxation, and had married it to population, which was quite a different spouse. Perhaps our forefathers, full of old testament wisdom, foresaw 'that a Jacob who would labor seven years for a Rachel, if then rewarded with the Leah whom he didn't want, would labor another seven years for the Rachel he did want, and thus make a good provision for two— in other words, that the people might ultimately be represented in proportion to taxation in one house, and in proportion to population in another.

No statistics are taken in the United States nor in any State of the number of tax-payers. As the State, county and town taxes rest on property, none are payers of such taxes by virtue of being either producers or consumers. They consist of a well defined class whose property, real and personal, is assessed, and according to which assessment a bill is made out, for which if not paid the property is sold. The burden of the tax can not be transferred. Its whole "incidence" or loss falls on him who pays it. Federal taxes are another matter. The census enumerates carefully every other beast of burden. Illinois, however, in 1872, cast 426,882 votes; and in 1870, according to the census contained 395,937 persons whose occupations were enumerated, exclusively of those engaged in manufactures and transportation. Assuming that the voters and the persons whose occupations are enumerated in the census, including those engaged in manufactures and transportation, are about 425,000 persons, and that they are pretty nearly the same persons, notwithstanding a small proportion of the persons included in the enumerated occupations are females, we have a basis from which to estimate the number of tax-paying voters. The 153,646 farmers are all tax-payers and voters, and alone form two-fifths of the voters of the State. The 125,331 laborers, farm laborers and servants are so nearly all non-tax-payers, that we may assume there are not more than 5000 tax-payers among them all. Of carpenters, blacksmiths, merchants, shoemakers, teachers, clerks, wheelwrights, physicians, masons, millers, tailors, lawyers, students and inn-keepers, there are 56,868, of whom doubtless three-fourths, or say 40,000, pay taxes on real and personal property; these leave 40,000 unaccounted for, whom we refer to railroading, transportation, navigation, mining, manufacturing, politics, preaching, office-holding, crime and other parasitic industries, among whom we will assume that two-thirds are tax-payers. On this basis our payers of State taxes are,

Farmers,	-	-	-	-	-	-	-	153,646
Tax-paying farm laborers, other laborers and servants,					-		-	5,000
Tax-payers of the enumerated occupations,			-	.	-		-	40,000
Tax-payers of the non-enumerated occupations,			-		-		-	27,000
Total,		-	-	-	-	-	-	225,646

Or a little more than half the voters. The tax-payers of any State in the Union, if united, could probably carry it against the non-tax-payers by a small majority, though a census of the tax-payers or a new system of returns by the town assessors to the comptroller of the State, would be necessary to give to such estimates any trustworthy character.

But hitherto in this country, no issue has been joined on any large scale between the tax-payers and non-tax-payers. Until such an issue is joined, every tax-payer votes precisely as if he were a non-tax-payer. Occasionally in some local school district or town election the issue will be drawn.

Thus in a school district with which I was acquainted in an eastern State, there was a sudden influx of millionaires without children, whose personal property tax became an easy prey to the resident voter. The sudden thirst for learning displayed by the parents of that district could only be compared to the enthusiasm with which poor house contractors pursue works of charity for their own sake, or to the interest an Indian agent feels in clothing the naked. Extras and special courses were piled up until the mere tuition at that school amounted to $600 per pupil per year, or nearly as much as both tuition and board cost at Yale College. The lines were drawn at a school election, the question being whether the millionaires had any constitutional right to a surplus for the maintenance of their families, or whether the parents of the district had the power to vote all the incomes of the residents of that district to the support of the school in question, leaving to those who earned the incomes only a contingent remainder. The effect of the election was, to decide that if the millionaires would thenceforth devote about $250 per pupil per annum to the education of the suffering children of that district, they might retain the balance of their property. Your lecturer had been partially educated, some fifteen years earlier, in the same district, when the aggregate expense to the tax-payers for maintaining the same school was only about $3 per pupil per annum; and to this day he attributes most of his deficiencies in logic, embroidery, dancing, and in the use of the piano, the harp and the timbrel, and in German, Italian, and pure speculative philosophy, to the fact that he was born fifteen years too soon. He should have lived hereafter, when he could have had the benefit of $600 per year of other people's money without rendering any equivalent. How many times a day ought the Bible to be read in such a school at the point where it says "thou shalt not steal," to efface the influence of the fact that the very Bible they were reading and the building in which they were reading it were stolen?

In one of the counties of Illinois, in 1865, 36 voters had advanced $100 each to save the town from the draft. Shortly after they procured an act to be passed authorizing towns in that county which had not filled their quotas, to

levy a tax therefor. On the day after the act was passed, and before reading
its exact terms, these 30 voters, there being 95 voters in all in the town, got
together, called themselves a town meeting, voted themselves $3600 in bonds,
voted also a bonus of several hundred dollars to the town officers who issued
the bonds, and the bonds were issued and the tax actually levied on the whole
taxable property of the town,—when the courts intervened, and held the election
void, because the notice of election called for by the act had not been given.
It is a humane principle of our election law, that no tax-paying constituency
going down from Jerusalem to Jericho shall be set upon and stripped and beaten,
and left for dead upon the highway, without due notice of the intention of
the voting constituency being given,—for all robbery, to be legal, must be con-
summated in accordance with the sacred forms of the constitution! Our entire
scheme of voting aids to schools, railways, parks, canals, etc., is based on the
theory that the right to tax is in the voters, while the obligation to pay is in
the tax-payers, and that the tax-payer, as such, has no constitutional rights
which the voter is bound to respect.

William M. Tweed, by sending a barrel of flour and a ton of coal occasionally to the poor voters of his ward or to some small fraction of them, controlled
the non-tax-payers of the ward, and through them the tax-payers whose money
paid for the coal and flour, and through the ward he controlled the city, and
ultimately the disbursement of from $25,000,000 to $40,000,000 a year, or more
than thirty of our State governments combined were disbursing in 1860. In
the disbursements of these moneys for marble, upholstery, and services on its
public buildings, rings were formed which levied toll on the bills paid by
the city, in sums which soon made the members of these rings the recognized
princes and plunderers of the metropolis. Nearly every city in the country
does the same thing in a less degree.

Impracticable theorists who don't know how to make money under the
glorious institutions of a free country, slanderously call this stealing. It is
only the legitimate result of the sublime truth to the dignity of which the whole
American people have arisen, that A and B who pay no taxes can vote how
much tax C shall pay, and what shall be done with it when paid; and that because A and B are represented, therefore C is represented.

Taxation and representation to be inseparable must be proportionate and to
be proportionate, the entire expenses of our State government, say $4,000,000
ought under our present system of voting to be paid by a poll tax of $10 on
every voter. Every voter assumes in voting to dispose of about $10 of some-
body's money. If he has paid the $10 of State taxes, he, in voting, asserts the
lawful right of a proprietor to dispose of his own. If he has not paid the $10,
he, as a political free-booter, exercises in voting a power to dispose of another
man's money, which is a power without a right.

Lord Chatham, in 1775, in the speech attributed to him, but the standard
report of which is from the pen of Dr. Samuel Johnson, sneered at the notion
that his Majesty's commons of England could tender to his Majesty aid and
supplies from the money of his Majesty's commons of America. But the non-
tax-payers of America have never had any scruples in voting aids and sup-

plies to be paid by the tax-payers of America. The separation of the class that votes the tax from the class that pays it, by 3000 miles of ocean, is not the fact which constitutes the tyranny. A distant oppressor would be moderate in his demands in the degree that he was insecure in his tenure. He could at best only swoop down upon us like the eagle, bury his talons occasionally in the firstlings of our flock and bear them away. But if coiled in ten thousand anaconda folds around all our limbs, the despotism becomes intense in the degree that the despot is identified with his victim, until, in the final fierce embrace, rescue becomes impossible and both must perish together, or the serpent only will survive.

But, says the average American statesman, to-wit: the voter, (for American statesmen, like British poets, are born, not made,) "who is harmed by this theoretical injustice? Do the spots upon the sun, which only an astronomer sees, diminish its usefulness? And can not the eternal glory of our National escutcheon afford a few spots, by way of completing its resemblance to the exhaustless source of light and life which warms the universe? Don't American corn have longer ears with more rows on them, and don't American hens lay more eggs a day, and aren't a larger proportion of the eggs laid with a double yolk, and don't the American eagle soar higher, and the American hog root deeper, and the American rooster crow earlier and louder, and according to more correct principles of crowing, and don't the American soil breed more brains and more brawn, and more muscle and more nerve to the half acre, than is to be found under the enervating flag of any of the effete and crumbling monarchies and corrupting dynasties of the Old World? Can't we allow more public money to be stolen than any of the picayunish and impoverished treasuries of Europe could afford, and have more left to divide up among ourselves after it is stolen? Can't we employ five times as many public servants to render one-fifth as much public service at a given cost as any other nation on earth? And haven't we shed more of the blood and treasure of our own people in twenty years, than it has cost any other government on earth to maintain itself for a century? And can there be any doubt that a system of government which has cost the lives of millions to maintain, must be valuable in the degree that it is costly? Haven't we crushed the biggest rebellion the world ever saw, and isn't it as a general proposition true, that any government is valuable in proportion to the frequency and the bigness of the rebellions it is crushing, and the weight with which it can sit down on the conquered rebellions when they are crushed? And isn't it a proud satisfaction to know that 12,000,000 of people out of 40,000,000 who have been trying to escape from the blessings and get out from under the freedom of our glorious liberty can't do it, but have been pinned into the enjoyment of our common brotherhood and national unity by the national bayonet?

Leaving both the eagle and the buzzard to soar, we come down to a plain matter of fact inquiry, what have been the effects of awarding representation in America to mere numbers, leaving capital unrepresented?

In England, where capital, or essentially land, and the church, are exclusively represented in the House of Lords, and influence the election of five-sixths of the House of Commons, we are struck by the fact that no tax rests on land or accumulated capital of any kind, while throughout all the American State governments the entire burden of State and local taxes rest on land and accumulated values, and no tax whatever on earnings, incomes, processes or other incidents of industry. In England, equality and uniformity of taxation mean the equality of all persons in proportion to their incomes and earnings. In America, the same words mean the equality of all persons in proportion to the value of the implement with which they work, *i. e.* their accumulated capital. In England, not only is capital protected from taxation, but from spoliation. The solvent borrower who refuses to repay, must pay the cost of collecting the debt at law. In all the Western States, the lender who refuses to wait until the borrower is ready to pay, must pay the cost of the effort to collect, and hence, while in England a debt against a solvent debtor who refuses to pay is worth its face, in Illinois it is worth according to its amount from two-thirds to one-third of its face. In England, crimes against the property and the person are punished with a fidelity of which we know little. In Illinois the criminals are screened from justice with an infidelity of which the world knows much. Unemployed capital flows to England from all parts of the world for the security afforded by its banks and other credit institutions and its courts of justice. But he who has deposited his money in a Chicago bank, feels that he has cast his bread upon the waters, and may look for it with the same probability of finding it on the banks of the Thames or the Ganges,

"Or by the lazy Scheldt or Wandering Po."

Or wherever else the unfortunate cashier can get board without registering his true name.

A voice: How about the Bank of Glasgow?

Ans. The Bank of Glasgow failed through honestly made investments, though unwise ones. The directors were guilty, not of converting the money to their own use, but of appropriating it irregularly in modes designed to serve the interests of the stockholders. For this irregularity they have been convicted, and are now in prison, suffering the penalty of violated law. Moreover, the property of the stockholders has been seized to reimburse the depositors. But in Chicago, where banks without number have been scuttled of their deposits by their officers, who has been punished? And where are the stockholders who have redeemed the word of promise to the depositors? There are none such.

The American States, in their forty Legislatures, probably employ 6000 persons in making laws, all salaried,—as against the 600 to 1000 persons, none of whom are salaried, who make laws for the British Empire; hence our remarkable cheapness! Of these 6000 legislators, if our Western States may serve as a sample, hardly one in fifty is a lawyer; hence our remarkable skill! The general object and drift of all the legislation of these forty legislatures is to protect the non-tax-payers, who constitute the most manageable part of their constituency, from all taxes on earnings or occupations or consumption, from all assertion of rights on the part of tax-payers, from all collection of debts, and ultimately from all punishment of crime.

Hence, in England, where capital feels secure, it will render its aid to industry at 3 per cent per annum, while in Illinois, if asked to lend money on the same kind of bond and mortgage as would suffice in England or in New York, *i. e.* one which a resort to the courts is necessary to foreclose, it would probably ask 25 per cent., but if given a trust deed of most of the borrower's present property and a judgment note which it can at any moment convert into a deed of his future property, it will lend at from 8 to 15 per cent. But the golden treasure enters the State of Illinois under as close a guard as it would Turkey. First there is the fierce and flashing Bashi Bazouk, with drawn scimeter, who determines the question of the value of the property. He is a Pacha, not of three tails but of three per cent. Then there is the heavily sabred and moustached apostle of the Koran, known as the commercial agency, which is secretly consulted as to the moral and religious character of the borrower, and whether he has always paid previous loans without contest. Then there is the band of bearded pards or legal sharps who have been following the tortuous windings of the Illinois Legislature and Supreme Court for forty years in the joint efforts of these two bodies to help and relieve the debtor class by means of clumsy acknowledgment laws, homestead laws, provisions for appeal and for stays that are without cost, without security and without limit as to variety, tax laws which divest the title of both borrower and lender unless certain taxes are paid, redemption laws, and such an organization of the courts that during eleven months of the year in many parts of the State the collection of debt is suspended. To steer clear of all these obstacles the lender demands a deed of the debtor's present property and a judgment note against his future, such as no debtor would ever think of giving, save in a country whose legislature and courts had been "protecting" the debtor class for half a century. Relatively therefore, to a country in which capital is represented, Illinois pays from 3 to 8 fold interest for the privilege of so legislating as to make capital insecure. Give capital a representation in our legislature and it will be as secure in Illinois as in London. If as secure, it would be as abundant at 3 per cent. If abundant at 3 per cent. the manufactures for which we wait in vain, though we have every facility but capital, would come, converting Illinois into a Belgium, our Ottawas, Elgins, Rockfords, Peorias and Rock Islands into Birminghams, Manchesters, Leeds, Sheffields, where would be spun the great part of the cotton crop of the South, and where would be smelted the ores of Missouri and Superior, and where would be assayed the precious ores of the Rocky Mountains. For by a law that is irreversable, the cotton, ores and metals, costing but about one-sixth for transportation of what the breadstuff and coal essential to their manufacture cost to transport, would come here by the same law which caused Mahomet to go to the mountain, viz: that the mountain refused to come to him. If the representation of capital in Illinois would give it the security which it does in England, as I believe it would, it would add in a very brief period 10,000,000 of souls to the population of the State, and untold thousands of millions of dollars to its lands. Large sections of our State, and especially those whose future prosperity depends on the introduction of manufactures, are at a stand still for want of capital. Agriculture, seeking new lands to skin, drifts through them for the farther west. Capital examines them, but on inquiry at our banks learns that money is never loaned in this State to promote production,—the time required is too long, and the means for getting it back when loaned to promote production are too uncertain. It is only loaned on values produced, *i. e.* on grain in the bin, where it promotes speculation and exportation. If it goes further and inquires why capital is never loaned here to promote production, it learns that it is because, instead of laws for the collection of debts, we have only a system of laws for the encouragement of debtors in defrauding creditors; and if still further it inquires why the debtor class exercise this power, it ascertains that it is for the same reason that an Indian tribe would sustain scalping, viz: that the scalpers are in the majority.

Along with high rates of interest, as a consequence of the government by by an undisciplined mob, come low standards of public virtue and of personal dignity as exhibited in our literature, in our drama, in our social manners so far as they are affected by politics, and in the acquirements of our public men.

In literature, the class of European works in which persons of some dignity of social position and character figured, have given place in our markets to the writings of a class of American humorists, in which the humor, if analyzed, will be found to consist largely in such an association of slang expressions with refinement of sentiment as will flatter every American into the feeling that if his manners and language are boorish, the inference is irresistible that his heart is kind and tender, and his sentiments are a delicate admixture of poetry and honor. Mark Twain, Artemus Ward, Will Carleton, John Hay, Josh Billings, Orpheus C. Kerr, P. V. Nasby, Bret Harte, the Danbury News man, all agree in importing into literature for the delectation of American society such a hash of slang and refinement as will convey the impression that every man ignorant of grammar is the soul of chivalry. On the stage, the Danites, "Josh Whitcomb," "My Awful Dad," "The Two Orphans," "Our American Cousin," and nearly every play produced within twenty-five years past, has had one or the other of two aims,—either to prove that people of aristocratic birth and education are on the verge of idiocy, like Lord Dundreary, or are destitute of morals and of honor, while ruffianism of manners is the external garb of true fidelity and refinement of character,—in short, if you would meet the true gentleman, scratch the first ruffian or vagabond you come to, and *vice verse.* English society has gone far in toadying to its counts, earls and kings. But if its civilization suffers more from cringing upwards than ours does from fawning downwards, if its manners are worse affected by imitating the dignity of the great than ours from aping the vulgarity of the mean, then indeed science is wrong, and it is the sun which absorbs the light which opaque bodies send to it.

Looking at our social manners as affected by politics, we find the average American politician (for the manners which originated in the west are rapidly spreading over the east as well,) is treated by his constituents not in any sense as a gentleman, but with a mixture of the flunkeyism with which a lackey over-rates a nobleman with whom he is brought in contact, and the contemptuous familiarity with which a boor regards one on whom he is conferring the favor of his patronage. Illinois ignores the gentleman, Mr. Richard J. Oglesby, to patronize the favorite son, Major General Dick Oglesby; so of Bill Springer, Dick Yates, Dick Townsend, Josh Allen, Jack Logan, and formerly "Nancy" Arnold and "Long John." "Honest Old Abe" was at home in this kind of familiarity; so was the "Little Giant." Ohio has a "Foghorn" Allen, a "Gentleman George," and formerly had a Sunset Cox. The Wisconsin Legislature at its senatorial election had to inquire of its candidate whether his mother knew him as Matthew Hale Carpenter, or as Matt. Chandler of Michigan is "Zach," and Williams of Indiana is "Blue Jeans," and the gentle Colfax of the same State used to be known to his more presuming friends as the smiling "Sky." Even the commonwealths, while aspiring to the dignity of empires, also fall under the indignity of this species of slang nick-names which in the Old World is confined to thieves and the fish-markets. Thus Ohio is the Buckeye State; Indiana the Hoosier State; Illinoisans are "Suckers;" Wisconsin in her playful mood is "Badger," and Michigan is "Wolverine."

Had Lord Brougham represented Chicago in Congress, he would have been Long Hank, Earl Russell would have been Little Jack, Sir Robert Peel would have been plain Bob, like Ingersoll, and the Hon. John Bright would have been Jack Bright, like Logan, or if he changed his party, then "Dirty-work" Bright. Even the right Hon. William E. Gladstone would be compelled, when his sovereign, the mob, was pleased to be gracious in his cups, to hear himself styled "Bill," as Mr. Seward, with all his dignity, used occasionally to be.

These external signs of familiar contempt express the truth that Americans do not look upon their public men as anything more than winners in a game of chance. Americans have great reverence for the constitutions and systems of government which result in putting a certain class of men in public office, but they know that those men are almost never skilled, and are seldom trustworthy. In every American audience therefore, in which the wholesale incompetency of public officers is assumed and their corruptions denounced, the utterance will be applauded. But if you intimate that the institutions are at fault, the answer will be "no, the tree is perfect, only the fruit is corrupt." In three points, as a rule, the American citizen's faith is firmly rooted: First, that the constitutions of the United States and of each State, are divine. Second, that the aggregated opinions of a sufficiently large mass of people, though the opinion of each one may be of no value whatever, becomes the divine wisdom and never errs, and thirdly, that a divinely inspired people, acting through a divinely inspired constitution, perpetually elect to office a worthless set of rascals. Here we have a trinity, therefore, in which the father is divine and the son is divine, but the joint energy and operation of the two, as manifested in the practical politician, instead of being the Holy Ghost, is the Devil, and yet after this Devil has done his perfect work in the Legislatures and in Congress, the glamour or divine fog again descends upon it, and the people regard every actually finished product of the industry of these rascals while in office, as undoubtedly wise—i. e. the foot-prints of the Devil are consecrated ground!

The wholesale distrust felt by the people in the quality of our public officers is far more just and deserved than the faith they repose in the wisdom of our constitutions, or in the implicitness with which they assume that the aggregate ignorance of a sufficiently large number of utterly uninstructed persons, especially if their opinions be taken by ballot, becomes divinely illuminated with wisdom. Whatever qualities render a public man unlike the mass of the people in his views, retire him from office. The people naturally regard themselves as the fountains of political wisdom, and do not want any man at Springfield or at Washington whose views differ in the least on political questions from those which a man will arrive at who spends all but a few hours of every year in currying down his horse or selling his goods. The average American citizen really studies politics, generally by the aid of very incompetent teachers, about ten hours in the course of a year; but the only years in which his mind is flexible, or he is capable of learning anything, are those between seventeen and thirty. Very few of them ever admit a new political idea into their heads after thirty. The average voter's political knowledge may be summed up in the following pocket library:

Vol. 1.   America is the only country that was ever free.

Vol. 2.   The Democratic (or Republican, as the case may be,) party is the continued salvation of American freedom.

Vol. 3.   General Jackson is the Alpha and Omega of modern statesmanship.

Vol. 4.   Statesmanship consists in doing what a wayfaring man, though a fool, thinks is right, and which so accords with the common sense of common people, that the more foolish a man is the more clearly he sees it is right.

Vol. 5.   The only great questions now in politics are, polygamy in Utah and the grasshoppers in Nebraska. Both these should be abolished by an act of Congress.

Vol. 6.   There is some danger that the Catholics may get the upper hand, and in that event the Pope would capture Washington and put a crucifix on every school house. This is to be prevented by teaching everybody how to read, and nobody how to work.

Vol. 7.   I don't know exactly what free trade is, but whatever it is it is a good thing.

This being the substance of the average American voter's political knowledge, no statesman whose views differ materially from this fundamental creed can be sent either to Springfield or Washington. Our constitutions and this state of public opinion, combined, compel the class of minds which might become statesmen to settle down into feeders of pap, exhibitors of bugaboos, and distributors of sugar plums to political babies, i. e., into stump speakers. A stumper differs from a statesman as a king's jester differs from a poet laureate. A statesman studies the means which promote the prosperity and welfare of a nation, and advocates them, trusting only to the dignity and truthfulness of his position; but a statesman can have no existence if his recognition as such depends on the ratification of his views by an illiterate peasantry. The speeches of Burke, Fox and Sheridan, on the impeachment of

Warren Hastings, could never have been made on the stump. The presence of the cultured audience is as essential as that of the orator. A stumper, therefore, studies merely the tricks of words, the pretty stories, the coarse jests, the hackneyed anecdotes which will flatter his audience into the feeling that they are a god, and that the other political party is the devil, and so will hold and catch votes. A stumper must utter no unwelcome truth, must teach the people nothing, for all new truths offend us, but must tell whatever crudity or lie the people already believe, dressing it up in such fine language that the people shall barely recognize it as being the well-dressed echo of what they already think.

No more skillful or effective utterance was ever made on the stump than Mr. Emory A. Storrs' story of the last campaign, about an inflation of collaterals. It garnered thousands of votes into the Republican coffers. The committees feared to have Mr. Storrs touch the financial question for fear he would say something, for Storrs is as bright as the best, and if he said what he thought, his horns might demolish the entire china shop. But Storrs knows that sugar plums and soothing syrup are, in squally times, the best things for the infant mind, and that while each individual of the American public, in the specialty to which he had given his life's energies, might be matured and wise, yet that the aggregate judgment of that public, when applied to a subject like statesmanship, to which not one in a hundred thousand had given attention, would be infantile. Thus compelled, the more able a man to be a a statesman, if statesmanship were required, the more certain he is to be a stumper, if only pap and sugar plums for babies are required.

Here is the Republican party arraigned by its adversaries for having crudely gone to work to force a paper dollar, of which there were say $100,-000,000 in circulation, up from a value of 70 cents each to a value of 100 cents each, in gold, knowing that the process would inevitably involve the reduction of all the other values in the country, of which this dollar was the purchasing agent, by the same percentage of value that was added to the paper dollar. By whatever distance the scale containing the dollar rises, the scale containing the commodities which buy the dollar must fall. There are $35,000,000,000 of values to be reduced 30 per cent., and $700,000,000 values to be raised 30 per cent., $12,000,000,000 of values are to be taken out of the other property in the country, in order that the instrument of exchange by which those values are measured may be made worth 30 per cent., or $300,-000,000 more. It was the repetition of the graceful idea of keeping the goose that we are roasting stationary, and having the stove and the fire and the house revolve around it; or as if in the old times, when the king's foot was the standard of measurement, the nation had come upon a king whose foot, though very graceful and useful otherwise, was only seven inches long, and had devoted five years to gradually pulling his foot out to the requisite length. Had a merchant discovered that his yard stick was too short, he would have retired it and substituted another of full length, or if his pound weight was too small, he would throw it under the counter and substitute another of full size. So Russia and Austria, finding, twenty years after their wars with

Napoleon had ended, that the paper currency of the one was worth but 24 per cent. of its face and that of the other but 60 per cent., both provided for retiring the old currency and substituting a new one worth par from the date of its issue, and for the payment of all debts in the old currency which were incurred in the old, or if payment were made in the new currency, then reducing the nominal amount so as to maintain the equation of actual values, and not make the debtor pay the creditor from 40 to 70 per cent. more value than he had agreed to pay. In this way these two effete monarchies resumed specie payments in a month, without deranging the values of all the property in both empires, or so much as disturbing the price of a pea nut to the value of a hair, without making the fire and the residence revolve around the goose that was being cooked, and without placing the foot of the sovereign people in the vise and rack, and pulling it out amidst the groans and yells of the suffering sovereign, from a length of seven inches to a length of twelve inches. But the glorious Republican and Democratic parties raise too much brains to the acre to care for any financial examples afforded by the effete despotisms of the old world, and so they combine to resume by a plan which will set all the values in the country toppling and falling like rows of bricks upon each other, so that production will be as nearly paralyzed as human ingenuity can render possible, by the fact that for years every product will continue to sell for less than the cost of producing it; for the Republican and Democratic parties combined had resolved, as a political truism, that the dollar, with which all other things were purchased, might be given a purchasing power relatively to all other things of 30 per cent. more, without any other thing losing any part of its power to purchase dollars. Hence, production was palsied, capital fled into the bank vaults with terror, labor roamed on the highways, fools everywhere talked finance, and the busiest bees in the bucket were the registers in bankruptcy and the hangmen. While the wind that resulted in the whirlwind was being sown, the Democratic party had its cheeks as full of wind as the Republican. But when the whirlwind came, then the Democratic party, like Adam of old, pointed to the woman and said: "The Republican party she did take, and gave to me, and I did eat also." In this dilemma, what the campaign committees want is soothing syrup. The Great American Baby has been having his foot stretched by the medical bears, and Mr. Storrs must explain to the dear, great, vast body politic, with the dear, small, little, tiny brain inside of it, that it mustn't kick the doctor up to where corn is worth $2 a bushel, nor upset the nurse, but must just open its little mouth and shut its little eyes, and receive from the Hon. and eloquent Emory A. Storrs something that will make it witty, and wealthy, and wise.

Then Mr. Storrs begins by telling the Great American Baby that he, Storrs, don't know anything about finance, which makes the baby feel comfortable, for the baby don't know anything about it either, and don't want to. Then Storrs tells the Great American Baby that he has been trying to borrow, and the baby now loves Storrs truly and deeply, because the baby has been trying to borrow an extra pair of lungs to howl with while the medical bears were stretching its foot. "Now," says Storrs, "I went to Coolbaugh, which being interpreted means Banker, and asked him if there was plenty of money to lend. Coolbaugh answered, 'slathers of it.'" Thereupon, the Great American Baby sweetly opens its dear, little, tiny eyes, and wonders how it could have hurt so to stretch its financial foot, when the banks all had plenty of liniment in their vaults, and modestly asks Mr. Storrs why it didn't get the benefit of any of the all-healing ointment. "Just the point," says Storrs. "I asked him for some of it—about $5000 would do—and Coolbaugh asked me for my collateral." Here the Great American Baby, with a precocious stare, asks if "collateral" is the bottle that keeps the ointment from spilling. "Just what I asked Coolbaugh," says Storrs. "Coolbaugh told me it was grain certificates —receipts for grain deposited by me in the elevators. Then, says I to Coolbaugh, if I owned grain deposited in an elevator, and which I could.sell for cash at any moment, or anything else that I could sell, would I come here to borrow?" "So," said Storrs to the Great American Baby, "I found there was plenty of money for all persons who have plenty of corn in the elevators. Ergo," says Storrs, "the article in which we need inflation is corn and other collaterals, not currency. People who have got plenty of corn can get plenty of money,·and people who don't own any corn, don't need any." Thereupon, the Great American Baby looked sweetly and confidingly up into the eyes of the Republican party, and gently murmuring, "Let Storrs, Hayes, Tom Jones or the devil run the country, its all one to me," went to sleep.

That is the best stump speech ever made, because the most powerfully sedative. If it has any rival, it would be the case of Nero fiddling while Rome was burning.

Institutions in which there is no better sorting of men for public office than that which can be made by the people in their primitive mass-meeting capacity, compel all candidates for office to be of the stumper grade—they must consecrate their lives to humbug. The same fate which would befall our other trades requiring special skill,·if the men who are to manage them were to be selected in town meeting, (and all universal suffrage is an enlarged town meeting,) befalls statesmanship. Suppose the question who were to run Giles' Bros. jewelry store next year, or Field & Leiter's dry goods store, or John Wentworth's farm, were put to popular vote, and Timothy Cronan, non-tax-payer, should take the place of Giles Bros. & Co., and bring the experience he had acquired in dredging to the sale of diamonds; could you trust the diamonds you were buying there any longer, or would not fraud be written over every counter? Suppose that, by the universal suffrage of South Chicago, the conduct of Field & Leiter's business could be transferred to some very intelligent politician, say to sheriff Kern, how would this kind of rotation affect the skill, how would the perpetual necessity of pretending to comprehend what they did not, affect the honesty with which the business would be conducted?

Statesmanship is the crowning achievement of human society—the adaptation of the largest experience, genius and learning to the comprehension of the wants of the grandest nation, when upheld and represented by hundreds of its foremost minds. It can not be the work of one man alone, nor can it emanate from, or be be inspired by, an uninstructed mass of ignorant men,

—4

though they number by countless millions. No possible aggregation of ignorance, however extended or unanimous, becomes wisdom. The very nation in
which it is to be exhibited must form an arena worthy of its power. It must
rise towards its pinnacle, upheld by the support of a vast aristocracy of intel-
lect and of merit. Each person who assumes to fill a niche in its temple,
must devote his life to the sublime study of the true wants, weaknesses,
interests, powers, needs, capacities and forces which combine to constitute
the mighty sweep and current of the nation's being; to the great work of
amending individual judgments by exhibiting to them a judgment more com-
prehensive and more nearly universal; and of reconciling the conflict of interest and passion which disturbs the superficial minds that are delving for
ores around the base of life's vast altitudes, by towering above them into the
eternal spaces where law makes known its unity, and undisturbed philosophy and reason forever reign.

Human law is the correction of individual errors, by conforming human
conduct to the higher reason of the aggregate of cultured minds. Statesmanship is the reconciliation of social conflicts of interest and passion, by unfold-
ing to the contending parties the broader view wherein is always discernible
the harmony of interests. Think you that such a work requires less preparation than to make a watch or to sell a diamond? No man is fit to make a law
on any subject who does not know what the legislation and adjudication on
that subject for 2500 years have been, and their effects. No man is fit to propose a public policy who has not made the observation of public policies in all
nations his study, and the evolution of public policies in his own country both
his study and his profession. And yet we regard a nomination to Congress as
a thing that any successful seller of tape can have sent to his door, like his
green groceries, if he pays for it.

The highest forms of statesmanship must be in part inherited. All their
materials can not be matured in one generation. The William Pitt who over-
threw Napoleon would have lacked the force of will at sixty, had he been
required to wait until that period for the opportunity, and he would have
lacked the opportunity at twenty-five, had he been compelled to crowd up between the people as a stumper. Therefore, Democratic institutions can produce no William Pitts, because they supply no Lord Chathams. whose prestige
can lift their sons at twenty-five into opportunities of statesmanship. A century of the American Republic has never produced one political leader who
was also, like Macauley, a historian, or like Lord Derby, a classic scholar,
or like Disraeli, a leader also in the world of letters and in the social world.
Nor could the present Disraeli have attained this three-fold mastery over
society, over literature and over politics, if required to work his way upward
on the American stump. Three generations were required to produce such
a success: the first, by accumulating the wealth, rescued him from the necessity of devoting his life to the lower ambitions; the second, by accumulating
the scholarship, endowed him early with what other men had done. The
present Disraeli's success began where that of his sire left off. The qualities
which would enable him to fill the three-fold position, viz: those of gentleman,

scholar, and man of genius, would shut him out of a seat in any one of our State Legislatures. Being a gentleman, he would not solicit or barter for or buy the votes of the political bummers and strikers of his district, without which he could not receive the nomination. Being a scholar, his opinions would sever him from sympathy with the crudities of which the political ignorance of the mass of the voters of his district would consist, and he could not represent them without being on their plane. Being a man of genius, he would perceive, clearly, how futile was the effort to make a government by the lower classes result in a wise government, and would have nothing to do with it, unless it were in the capacity of a revolutionist.

The reign of the race of stumpers, the product of American institutions, began with the war of 1812, prior to which the country, in gratitude for the aid received from royal and aristocratic France, in 1778, under King Louis, La Fayette and Rochambeau, had broken out into a fervor of sympathy with the French Republic, under Robespierre, Marat, and Danton, which culminated in rendering us allies to the Napoleonic despotism, for which we fought under the banner of free ships, until its overthrow compelled us to receive peace at the hands of the allied powers of Europe; though most Americans, for fifty years afterward, thought that the battle of New Orleans, fought five weeks after the treaty of peace was signed, settled the conflict. Our next conspicuous act of infatuation and stumperism was the beginning, made in 1820, and continued until 1860, in treating the slavery question sentimentally and passionately on both sides, like a mob or a nest of fishwives, while the Czars of Russia were treating it coolly, dispassionately and economically, forecasting, by their legislation, as early as 1828 to 1830, the final abolition of the slavery of four and a half times as many slaves as disturbed our peace; so that while we precipitated emancipation on the subject race unadvisedly, at a cost of half the values in the country, to-wit: of $9,000,000,000, and of 1,000,000 lives, Russia perfected a greater result advisedly and gradually, without the cost of a dollar or a sigh.

The crushing, under Andrew Jackson, of the United States Bank, founded by Hamilton, and the subsequent war against institutions of credit and against credit itself, are exactly on a par with the North American Indian's hostility to fences, farms, herds and all private property. The Indian hates a farm as he does a telegraph pole, because it expresses something he don't understand, and Jackson, the Indian fighter, just one grade in advance of the Indian in statesmanship, and no more, hated a bank for the same reason, because he was as densely ignorant of political science as an Indian is of electric science.

For twenty-five years the force of our nation has been expended in proving that the majority of the people in one section can play the Cæsar over a minority in another, and hold them within their grasp, however unitedly they may wish themselves out of it, may abolish their institutions and constitutions, and revolutionize their social life, without giving any other explanation of the reason than that they have the power, *i. e.*, without attempting to show that such an exercise of authority redounds to the greatest good, either of the con-

quered people or of the conquerors. To all these results stumperism is fully
equal, and statesmanship is not requisite.

Imagine the ascendency of capital in the Legislature of Great Britain taken
away, by abolishing the House of Lords and delivering the country over to
universal suffrage, and the same war upon the banks, capital, credit and
finances of the country, which has occurred here, would transpire there, for
the class of men who are ignorant of political economy make war on all forms
of public and private credit, as instinctively as the Chinese oppose railroads,
or the Indian, fences. By destroying the security of capital they would send
rates of interest up to 8 to 12 per cent., would destroy England's ascendency
in manufactures and finance, and would reduce her in a few years to a Republic without external possessions, and numbering, perhaps, half her present
population.

The people who have exhibited a greater genius for government than any
other in history, were the Roman. For eight hundred years they ruled the
political world, virtually giving rise to both ancient and modern civilization.
So long as the Roman aristocracy, through the representation of capital in her
system of voting, were able to counteract the folly of the alien mob of people
of all nations which came under their sway, Rome ruled herself and the world.
Her demoralization and downfall as a political power were directly the result
of withdrawing power from capital and giving it to numbers; and as if on
purpose to demonstrate that the Roman aristocracy still retained its vigor
when it had lost its control over the State, it transferred its control to the
church, and under the name of Italian Cardinals the same Roman blood has
swayed christendom for sixteen centuries, and now, with a vigor as of peren-
nial youth, rules the consciences of 180,000,000 souls. The key to this ruler-
ship is to be found in the fact that Rome, both in its secular and religious
empire, governed from above downwards, impressing the genius and will of
the capable upon the dullness and inertia of the incapable. Twenty-five years
of government from the people upwards, by universal suffrage, the pews ruling
the priests and the priests the bishops, would demolish the Roman Church as
it did the Roman State.

In the Republic of Rome there were three modes of voting, which distinguished, respectively, the infancy, the ascendency and the decay of the State.
In the earliest mode, known as the *Comitia Curiata*, only the patricians or aristocracy voted, but the vote of one patrician was equal to that of another, as in
the British House of Lords. From that, Rome passed to the more complex vote
by centuries, known as the *Comitia Centuriata.* The people were divided at
the census into six classes, according to their wealth. As the purchasing
power of Roman money can not be accurately expressed in modern money,
it may be proximately accurate to say that all worth upwards of $1,000,000
were in the first class, and had thirty-five parts in a hundred of the voting
power of the State, and furnished thirty-five hundredths of the army and the
treasury.   Those worth less than $1,000,000, and more than $500,000, were
in the second class, and furnished one-quarter of the army and of the revenue,
and enjoyed one-quarter of the voting power. An absolute union of the first

and second classes, therefore, could carry any measure, and the vote of the other classes needed not to be taken. If, however, a vote of the first and second classes failed to exhibit a majority of the whole, then the third class, worth say $100,000, or the fourth, worth $50,000, or the fifth, worth $10,000, or the sixth, worth $500, would be consulted. In practice, the $500 class was seldom consulted, and I think it is literally true that the votes of persons who have never been able to accumulate $500 in property, upon any question of State policy, may safely be taken last.

Under no system of government has the inseparability of taxation and representation been preserved and vindicated in so logical, perfect and masterly a way as in this Roman system of voting by centuries. The right to cast a certain voting power, grew out of the possession of a corresponding amount of assessed capital, and carried with it inseparably the obligation to contribute a corresponding ratio of the army and the revenue. It was this identity of taxation and representation, this system of voting by centuries, which advanced Rome to be the ruler of the world.

The third system of voting, known as voting by tribes, or *Comitia Tributa*, admitted the plebeians, freedmen, aliens and non-property-holders to vote on an equality with the aristocracy, whereupon, of course, the aristocracy stopped voting altogether, and the crazy Roman mob were the saddled asses on which the Cæsars rode into power; thus making universal suffrage, when divested of the counteracting influence of capital, the stepping stone to the complete abolition of all suffrage, and the subversion of the Republic by the Empire, which, in its turn, was ground to powder between barbaric force and religious superstition. But to the end of time it will stand recorded that the ascendency of the Roman race, as well as of the British, over the world, (and they have been the two governing races of the world,) has been due to the joint ascendency given to capital and numbers in their constitutions—or as Mr. Calhoun would express it, to the fact that their constitutions secured the concurrent assent of the majority of property, as well as of the majority of polls, to all policies.

On this subject no American statesman has thought to any purpose, so far as I am aware, except Mr. Calhoun, in his celebrated disquisition on Government. He may, perhaps, have been led to think of it by the reflection that the peculiar form of capital in which the wealth of the South was so largely invested, viz: slave capital, would be that which a despotism of mere numbers would be the first to abolish, whereas, had the capital of the country had a veto on the action of numbers, there can be no doubt that the extinction of slavery, instead of being the subject of a sentimental, passionate and bloody war, would have been as gradual and peaceful in this country as in Russia, and would have occurred just as fast, and no faster, than the pecuniary interests of both the master and the slave would have combined to render it mutually desirable, and the 1,000,000 men lost in abolishing it would have been alive, and the $9,000,000,000 spent in destroying it would have been saved. Whatever were Mr. Calhoun's inducements to reflect upon the insecurity of capital under a despotism of mere numbers, he took the ground in his remarkable disquisition on Government, that governments are constitutional and enduring only when they combine the concurring majorities of each of the distinct forces which go to make up the power of society. If the priesthood and religion really govern society, as they do in Turkey, Italy, Spain and Mexico, then they will have power enough to overturn any State in which they are not represented. If the landholders are the chief social force, as in Germany, France and England, then a government which ignores the landholders, and rests, for instance, on the priests, must fall or give place to one in which the landholders are represented. If the army and the aristocracy are the chief forces in the State, as they were in Rome, then their ascendency must be acknowledged in the constitution, or they will overthrow the constitution which ignores them. And finally, if the church, and the army, and the landholders and capitalists, all cease to be a force in the State, as they do in communities where capital is equally diffused, and there are a hundred sects, and no standing army exists, there numbers become a ruling power, and any constitution which fails to respect them will fall.

Mr. Calhoun defined a despotism as being a government which attempted to rule society exclusively by one of its forces, whether such force were the church, the army, the landholders, or mere numbers, *i. e.*, the mob. He defined a constitutional government as one which provided for gathering up and representing the views of each of the ruling forces of the State in a co-ordinate branch of the Legislature, in such a manner as to give to its united voice a veto on the action of the other forces of the State. · If numbers, therefore, were represented in the lower branch of a State Legislature, and capital in the upper, he called this a government by concurring majorities, *i. e.*, the majority or voice of numbers concurring with the majority or voice of capital; whereas, if numbers merely elected both branches of the Legislature, the government not having provided itself with any machinery by which it could take the views or listen to the voice of capital, would be, as to capital, a hostile, uncompromising despotism, deaf to the voice of persuasion, and carrying out all its decrees by force. Mr. Calhoun pointed out, very clearly, the tendency which the majority would have, not only to tyrannize over the minority, but to vest so large a share of power in its individual chieftain, the President for instance, as would expand his powers into those of an Emperor, while still wearing the title of a President, and would enable him to override both the will of the Legislature, of the judiciary, of his constitutional advisers, and of his own party. The careers of Andrew Jackson, of Abraham Lincoln, of Andrew Johnson, and of Mr. Hayes, illustrated, with different results, this tendency of the leader to absorb in himself the despotic power accorded to his party. Jackson, of his individual will, abolished the bank. Lincoln, of his individual will, inaugurated the war for the Union, and converted it into a war for emancipation. Johnson attempted to reconstruct the South without consulting Congress or the people, and was defeated. But Hayes, of his individual will, released the South from further Federal subjugation.

It will thus be seen, that, according to Mr. Calhoun's definition, our State governments are all unconstitutional despotisms, in which both political parties combined, and the entire State government, represent but one of the forces of society, there being no provision for affording an authoritative expression to either capital, or culture, or character, or experieuce.

Mr. Calhoun did not intimate that he thought there were any other forces in American society so strong as to need representation in our forms of government, except those of numbers and capital, nor did he outline the system of voting, either by the people or in the Legislature, whereby the representation of capital, concurrently with numbers, could best be secured. The modes of represeuting capital, either in Europe -or in the Republics of Greece and Rome, are uot fitted to deserve favor here. The nobleman in the English House of Lords is in uo strict sense a represeutative of any body's capital but his own, nor are his sympathies identified with the interests of that portion of the capital of the country invested in mauufactures, banking or trade, except as some of his tenants may be manufacturers, bankers or traders, but only with that portion invested in land. This has made the British House of Lords, while a politic, compromisiug, and adroit, yet, in the main, a narrow, bigoted, and unrepresentative body, and has caused the power to pass from it to the House of Commons, whereas, if the House of Lords were so re-organized as to represent, logically and by proxy, the entire capital of the country, it would speedily return to an equality in influence with the House of Commons.

We are now prepared to outline the mode in which, in American Legislatures, representation might be given to capital. Let every State and city in this country, for the purpose of electing the upper branch of its Legislature, be treated as a financial corporation, for such in fact it is, in which the integral unit to be voted upon, corresponding to a share in the corporation, is the dollar of taxable property. Let every man cast a vote corresponding either to the number of dollars on which he pays taxes, or if the taxing system should be changed, as it probably would under such a method, from a tax on capital to a tax on iucomes and earnings, then to the amount of taxes he pays. Thus much would be fundamental. The other details would be matters of expediency. If the representation of the majority, only, of capital were deemed expedient, then a prescribed number of members would be voted for, and a prescribed amount of capital must vote for each member to perfect his election. The entire capital of the State being a trifle over $2,000,000,000, if the number of members were fifty, then each member elected would have to be voted for by a little more than one-fiftieth of $1,000,000,000, or by $20,000,000. If majorities of capital only are sought to be represented, as they are of numbers, the members of the house representing capital might be elected at one time, and serve for a given period, as our present members representiug numbers are and do. If, on the other hand, instead of the majority of capital only being represented in the Legislature, it is preferred that the whole capital of the State should be represented, then there might be no prescribed number of members in the upper house. Every tax-paper might be left free to vote in person or by proxy, for the instances in which they would care to vote in person would be very few, and the weight of the vote of a single tax-payer would be very small in a body in which the entire capital of the State voted.

- Suppose, for instance, that all the railroads in the State, combined, should send their proxies to one member, he would cast a vote for $130,000,000 of property, in a body wherein the other tax-payers, mostly agricultural, would cast a vote on $1,870,000,000, the railroads having about one-fourteenth of the power in the capitalist branch of the Legislature. Who believes that the railroads of Illinois, Pennsylvania or New York, where they have no legitimate representation at all, and their only weapon is bribery, do not wield a power greater than one-fourteenth of the aggregate political power of the State? The power they attain unrepresented, by corruption, is far greater than the power they are legitimately entitled to; but as at present purchased, it is a power which will be exercised more and more each year by local Illinois and New York railroad rings, to rob both the people of the State and the foreign stockholders in these railroads.

But to return. If the entire capital of the State, and not merely the majority of capital, is designed to be represented, then each tax-payer should have the privilege of voting, either in person or by proxy. There would be no general election of members of the upper house, but proxies might be forwarded to the book-keeper of the Senate, by mail or otherwise, as checks are sent in to a bank, each proxy authorizing a given person to cast the vote of a given tax-payer, in form thus: "John Smith, Chicago, votes for Richard Roe, of Springfield, for Senator; taxable property, $20,000." The book-keeper of the Senate would make up each day or week the account current of each member and of all the proxies, verifying it, as to the right of the voter to vote on the amount of capital which he purported to vote upon, by the returns which would be required to be forwarded each year by the assessors and collectors of taxes of towns to the State comptroller, showing the amount of taxes paid during the preceding fiscal year by every tax-payer in the State. Each member voting would not, as in the British House of Lords, cast a vote equal to any other, but he would cast the vote of the property represented by the sum of his proxies, whether it were $1,000,000 or $500,000,000. Theoretically, therefore, if the entire property of the State chose to vest in one individual the power of a veto on the action of the mere numerical majority, it could do so, but it would be very unlikely to vest such a power, except in some person whose single judgment would be unimpeachable. And, on the other hand, should a member lose the confidence of his constituency, they could, by the next morning's mail, forward the proxies heretofore held by him to a new or another member, and so, in a day, retire from power the one who had proved recreant to his trust. Such a system would involve some book-keeping, but the quantity would be insignificant compared with that of a bank or clearing-house, and, as a result, the entire capital of the State would each moment be represented by a member responsible, from day to day, to his constituency. Compared with such a system for the representation of capital, the British House of Lords is as clumsy and antiquated as a Mexican plow, and even the Roman method of voting by centuries was less logical.

The representation of capital would practically accomplish most of the results which would be reaped from a representation of culture and character, yet it would be quite practicable to give a representation to the latter. It might consist, in part, in regarding certain degrees of official experience, and certain classes of services rendered to science and literature, as the equivalent (for voting purposes) of a given amount of property. Such, in outline, would be Mr. Calhoun's system of government by concurrent majorities. What would be the popular objections to it may be easily conceived. "It would create a House of Lords in every State," says one. "It would increase the inequalities of society," says another, "making the rich richer and the poor poorer," says a third. "It would break down the common school system," says a fourth, "for the property holders would never vote the taxes necessary to educate the poor." "Why, the women and the corporations would vote away our liberties," says the hiccoughing statesman from "Biler avenue."

The best way to overcome these objections is to let them die. Answering them keeps the life in them. They are exactly of the character of the objections which the American Indians entertain to fences, to private property, and to the monopoly every man and woman asserts to the exclusive possession of his or her own scalp.

It is idle, however, to suggest, as a possible reform, any change in our body politic if the change involves for its feasibility conditions which do not exist in our body politic. We might as well descant on an improvement in the health of our planet which is to be brought about by transferring to it the atmosphere of the planet Saturn, as to discuss some renovation of American institutions, which the American people, or a majority of them, can not be induced to desire. But it is not safe to affirm too positively in advance what the American people can or can not be induced to desire. Two years before the Southern States were reconstructed on the basis of impartial suffrage and equal political rights, as between the two races, a distinguished U. S. Senator and Chairman of the Judiciary Committee, whose judgment as to the condition and progress of public sentiment was as accurate as that of any politician or statesman extant, informed me that he had conferred personally with all the men whose votes were necessary to reconstruct the South on the basis of negro suffrage and equal political rights, and that not one of them would vote for it under any conditions. I replied that I thought the course of events would oblige them all to vote for it within two years, including himself,—and they all did. I have known American statesmen who would telegraph in great haste from Washington to Chicago one week that a certain policy was not to be advocated, as it would ruin the party and the country, and would take the very next train for Chicago in order to get here in time to address a mass meeting in Court House Square in favor of the same policy, and this, not once, but frequently. He who would foresee what public opinion will be five, ten or fifty years hence, can not learn it from the clamor of to-day's mob on the streets, nor from the talk of traders and bankers. He must grasp the wants and needs of society, and judge from the laws of demand and supply, which govern the rise of institutions as they do the price of wheat. The progress of a nation toward wealth implies a wide and ever increasing differentiation of fortunes and large accumulations of capital under single control. This process is rapidly going on in America and is already creating aggregations of capital too powerful to submit to the despotism of a communistic voting system which is liable at any moment to endanger or abolish any form of private property or credit against which the cry of demagogues may direct the passions on the cupidity of the mob.

I concede that the representation of capital as a distinct integral force in the State, worthy to counteract the impetuosity and ignorance of mere numbers, will not be brought about until one or the other of the two political parties, contending for the government of the country on the basis of mere numbers, shall be driven to advocate it as the means of either atta ning to power or maintaining itself in power. It was from this motive that the Democratic party opened the gates of the constitution to the alien, and the Republican party opened the same gates to the negro. Will any political party ever find it necessary to the maintenance of its hold on power to open the gates of the constitution to the tax-payer? If not, the tax-payer will never be represented, and all political parties will continue to hold the fundamentally rotten proposition which now underlies our State constitution: that A, B and C, being the majority, can divide the garment of D among them and cast lots for his vesture, because they outnumber him. In the Northern States, the Republican party, by its antecedents and proclivities, would be most likely to become the champion of capital, for several reasons, viz: first, that at present by far the greater majority of its voters are tax-payers, and the actual and relative power of the men who now constitute the bone and sinew of the Republican party would be increased five fold by the measure. Secondly, the measure would draw to the Republican party the vast majority of the capitalists of the large cities who, either by the free trade or pro-slavery proclivities of the Democratic party, have been Democrats. The country is liable at any moment to drift into an exigency wherein the Republican party, driven to the wall, could only, by becoming the champion of the square and honest representation of capital in one branch of every Legislature and of every city council, recover its position and maintain itself in power. And now thirdly, the tendencies toward agrarian, socialistic and communistic legislation are such that its antidote, the representation of capital has got to be discussed. However much we may deprecate it, one or the other of the two political parties will be driven to it, and in the Northern States that party will be likely to be the Republican—at the South, the Democratic. The scum of society would meet the proposition with a howl at first, and would threaten its advocates with the lamp post and with assassination. But the votes of one-half of this scum could be bought in its favor for $10 each, and without the votes of any of them the measure could be carried if the tax-payers unite upon it. In our city governments, which, under our present system, are a rude and barbarous failure, the representation of capital in one branch of the city council would be of inestimable value. In the city of London, where the property qualification prevails, no member of the Board of Aldermen has ever allowed his note to go to protest, and in the city of Liverpool the bankruptcy of a member of the Board of Aldermen vacates his seat. But New York and Chicago have been governed ever since they were cities by bankrupts whose names often are not to be found in the city directory, still less on the tax list, and the circumstance of one not a bankrupt serving in the city council would be regarded as a capital joke. The Chicago *Times*, last fall, published the amount of taxes paid by all the members of the Cook County Democratic County and Congressional Convention at about $27, and all those paid by the Republican Convention at less than $70. All the men whose votes disposed of the elective offices for 500,000 people did not pay $100 of taxes. Hence, New York never knows, within from $20,000,000 to $40,000,000, how much her debt is, and Chicago never knows how much of her debt is valid. Both cities are governed by their vagabonds. In the Southern States the Democratic party are the natural defenders of the rights of capital, and while there would be nothing in such a measure which would tend to disfranchise any man on account of color, the concurrent representation of capital with numbers would rid every Southern State of all fear of negro domination until such time as the blacks should attain to a considerable share of the capital of the State. Indeed, under this system, the upper branch of any Southern State Legislature would be necessarily white, or white with the exception of one member, as the entire tax-paying capital owned by negroes in any State, except Louisiana, if concentrated upon one candidate, would be hardly or barely sufficient to elect him.

Capital seeks permanency and skill, and abhors change and incompetency. The representation of capital would impart permanency to the profession of the statesman, and when adopted in conjunction with executive responsibility, it would demand and develop skill. Intelligent minds in all ages have agreed that an aristocratic form of government developed the highest deliberative capacity and executive skill. It was supposed by many that democracy in government was conducive to honesty, but our American experiment has exploded all that and shown that democracy is only conducive to honesty when it is counteracted by an aristocratic influence. All the unfortunate tendencies to misgovernment which I have traced as the direct result of the non-representation of capital would be cured by its representation. Dishonesty would be eliminated from politics, for nothing but dishonesty can logically be expected from a system in which robbery is the chief corner-stone. Dignity would be restored to politics, for nothing but vulgarity can be expected from a system which fails to recognize the very first quality of virtue cognizable by the human conscience, viz: the virtue of the man who acquires, relatively to the vice of him who merely and frivolously dissipates. Our institutions, for the first time in our history, would be founded upon justice, for there is no justice in confiscation nor in unqualified communism. We should be able to retain in the public service statesmen who ventured to draw their inspiration from higher sources than the clamor of the liquor saloons, and the scarcely more intelligent clamor of a superficial and often venal press. In conjunction with a responsible system of government, by dissolvable legislatures and resignable ministries, it would eliminate from our political system the power of the caucus and the convention, those great conspicuous shams which overtower all the minor forms of American incompetency and knavery. It would introduce into our social fabric that due antagonism of centrifugal and centripetal forces, of capital and labor, of aristocracy and democracy, which are but illustrations of the divine truth that all enduring forms of action, all forces which contain the elements of perpetuity, all constitutions which are to outlast the centuries, all laws which are to range in harmony with the infinite unity of law, must be, not the mere expression of a solitary force, but the result of a union of antagonistic forces. For the unity of law is as perfect in politics as in chemistry. Oxygen without nitrogen is death. Nitrogen without oxygen is death. No two substances antagonize each other more powerfully or unite more firmly. So of gravitation and cohesion, matter and soul, liberty and law, and so finally of capital and labor, of aristocracy and democracy. If a divine truth underlies the statement that no government can be permanent in which these two principles are not jointly represented—if a government by mere numbers is inherently as much a despotism as a government by one—then he who advocates this divine truth need not wait long for its apprehension. He is at best but a yard or two in advance of the mighty tread of the millions.

> For humanity sweeps onward. Where to-day the martyr stands,
> On the morrow crouches Judas, with the silver in his hands.
> In the van the stake is ready and the lurid faggot burns,
> While the hooting mob of yesterday in silent awe returns,
> And gathers up the scattered ashes into history's golden urns.

I humbly trust we are approaching an epoch of Constitutional Invention, Investigation and Reform. The deep distrust, profound, restless and dangerous as the heavings of the ocean in its wrath, which pervades American society in all its highths and depths, indicates that we are living in a period wherein fetich worship is dead, and the constitutions bequeathed to us by our ancestors must be judged like the trees, by their fruits,—like the mechanism, by the harmony and fitness with which it accomplishes an excellent and perfect result. To the examination of such questions we need to bring the broadest and most catholic spirit of scientific investigation, combined with the highest inspiration of patriotic rectitude. We need to study the constitutions of all States, for we may say of constitutions as Gœthe says of languages, "who does not know another, does not know his own." Let us expunge from public opinion that narrow stupidity which, instead of welcoming suggestions from every hand, says to the critic of our institutions, as but a few years ago it said to those who criticised slavery in America: "If you like other governments better, go and live under them." As if any class could do more honor to America than those who try to make it what it ought to be. None are competent for the work who are not willing to borrow from each nation and period every excellence which American institutions can receive, even as the religious Roman thought not his pantheon complete so long as the traveler from any clime failed to find there the god he worshiped. As a true American, I cannot rest so long as any excellence pertaining to any government or state of society is wanting in my own.

DRIFTING TOWARD COMMUNISM;

OR,

THE TENDENCY OF THE RULE OF NON-TAX-PAYERS TOWARD AGRARIANISM, DIS-UNION AND CIVIL WAR.

THE first fifty years of our national life were presided over by politicians who were not the product of our institutions, but the authors of them. They had been produced by preceding and mainly English civilization. Only within the last fifty years have our institutions been guided by the men whom they have produced. Now we begin to see their drift, and compare their net results with those produced under more aristocratic conditions. We can now approach our august sovereigns, the People, and discuss with them plainly whether they govern well. Two antagonistic forces compose society, the one called the lower or laboring or democratic or non-capital class, and the other the capitalist or aristocratic class. In generalizing two forces of such breadth and scope of operation, no name that could be given them would be just to each of their details. As when liberty and law, or science and religion, or the latter and philosophy are arrayed as antagonistic social and intellectual forces, virtues and crimes attach to each; truth and error lie involved in both. As the world of force consists of antagonistic forces, so the world of truth consists of the antagonistic intellectual conceptions of these forces, which we call ideas. A truth which purports to generalize many facts into one generic fact or law, is never presented with complete accuracy, until the truth that contradicts it is set down beside it; as the Roman conqueror, returning in triumph, was followed by two heralds, one of whom proclaimed him immortal, and the other warned him that he would die. Neither told him the whole truth, but the two combined, did.

In the perpetual conflict between aristocracy and communism, each has at times been religious or irreligious, useful or despicable, sane or diseased. No one phase of either is responsible for the sins or deserving of the merit of any other.

Communism, or the doctrine that all men should enjoy all, or nearly all things in common, is the theory of employing the aggregate power of the mass to promote the interest of the individual. It antagonizes individualism, which is the theory that the interests of all are best promoted when each one promotes his own. All private property, so far as it is protected by law, rests upon communism in one sense, since what we call the protection of the law consists in the right of the owner of property to call upon all citizens to protect him in its enjoyment. This right to the services of his fellow men is the essence of communism. Communism would use the many to benefit each. Individualism leaves each to benefit himself, believing that he thereby most benefits the many. Communism aims at Altroism or Benevolence. Individualism culminates in Egotism. Communism is mainly a creed, *i. e.* the assertion of a theory. Individualism is the all controlling fact that governs the business of life, and sways the springs and forces of human nature. Communism in government believes in numerical majorities, and would see no better mode of deciding whether God exists, than by a vote of "eight to seven." Individualism may condescend to buy or use majorities, but it can not believe in them. It believes in genius, destiny, rank, headship, blood, property, achievement, any machinery by which to bring the many incompetent under the guidance and energy of the competent few.

Communism, in the church, subordinates pulpit to pews; inspiration to the pay-roll; elects its own preacher, tries him for his offenses on its own standard, and if he merely sins against God, extends to him the forgiveness—of the congregation. But if he sins against the congregation, expels him. Individualism in religion asserts its own intuitions or inspirations, subordinates many to one, and makes that one a Paul, a pope or a Luther. Business has generally been left to Individualism. Worship has tended toward Communism. Both have their sphere. Wisdom lies in the perpetual balance of each against the other.

A thread of communism runs through history, from Plato and the building of the Jewish temple to the Paris rebellion and the Indiana divorce law. But the world has been ruled and run by its Cæsars and Bonapartes—its men of business, and not by its St. Simons and Fouriers. The Cæsars have been coarse in the gratification of their passions, but chaste in the enunciation of their theories. The communistic theorist, isolated through illrepute or poverty, has lived the life of an eremite while advocating license, thus sustaining the inconveniences of virtue and the odium of vice. Cæsarism, when not engaged in a debauch, advocates purity, at least for others. Communism dwells under a cloud of suspicious repute, on an actual average of licentiousness which would cut no figure were its creed sound. Perhaps this is because Cæsarism has ruled the world, while communism has only speculated on how it should be ruled. All governments vibrate between these two forces. But the governments and people of the United States of America tend more visibly than any other in modern times toward communism. DeTocqueville observed this forty years ago when he wrote of the despotism of public opinion, and the power which society asserts in America to compel each individual to agree with the mass.

Our Declaration of Independence is a gospel of communism. Its utterance "all men are created equal" is a half truth, the other half of which is "all men are created unequal" and ♦ endowed by their Creator with a capacity to serve each other proportionate to their inequality. The Declaration does not, as some suppose, assert the equality of men as to their political rights. The rights to life, liberty and the pursuit of happiness, are not political, but natural rights. The right to vote, hold office, enjoy a franchise, etc., would be political rights. If the right to the pursuit of happiness is inalienable, then no man can at any time be checked in doing that which he thinks will make him happy. If liberty is inalienable, no man can be imprisoned for crime. If life is inalienable, no criminal can be executed. Men derive their power of exchange and association from their inequalities. Whatever would make them equal would destroy the race by stopping commerce. Capital would hire nobody, wealth would cease to have value if each laborer possessed it. It is because the workman wants, that capital employs, and production goes on. Men that can make shoes make them for men that can not.. Men that can make laws make them for men that can not. Differentiation of functions or division of labor is as essential to the highest skill in government as in any other art. If it were possible in fact, as it only is in theory, for all men to make laws, then the laws which all men make would be as bungling as the shoes which each man might make.

No government ever derived its power from the consent of the governed. Under all, the governed have derived their power to express their consent from the concessions of the governors. History opens with the governing classes in the saddle, not with a compact by which they are invited to ride. Governments begin, not in the desire of the great to protect the humble, but in the aristocratic determination of the strong to use the massed power of the many for their own aggrandizement.

In Plato's ideal Republic, the government was to be aristocratic; only the educated were to make the laws, but the soil and its fruits were to be shared equally by all. One year's residence in the United States would have taught him that if property, which is inseparable from power, were equally shared by all, the educated would have no monopoly of law-making. The people desire law-makers who are more fluent than themselves, but not such as differ from them in their conclusions.

The State, says Plato, should set all men at work. The women, slaves and children should be the common property of the State; forgetting that what all men own, like the sea or the heavens, may have great utility or beauty, but no value; it can not be prized or loved. That which can not be mine I will not have. To share, to equalize property or affection is to abolish it. In its very dawn the principle of communism was hostile to marriage. Generally associated with some form of religious fanaticism, it has not been content with making property common to all, but has either established celibacy, community of wives, or polygamy. In a few instances only it has left the marital relation intact.

The sect of the Essenes, according to Neander, were contemporaneous with the Sadducees and Pharisees. Their doctrines were identical with those of Christ, though they are nowhere mentioned either by Jesus or by his disciples. They were purists in morals, and taught non-resistance, celibacy, prayer, fast-ing, humility and poverty, and were communists as respects property. Christ's own teachings concerning property were more communistic than his followers in later ages have been willing to admit. In the early church, all christians were communists, ate at a common board, and in joining the christian sect poured all their wealth into the common stock. The Carpocratians, an early christain sect, continued from the first to the seventh century to practice community of goods and of wives. All monasticism has been communistic as respects property. The clerical body, as well as the various religious orders, male and female, of both the Greek and Roman Catholic churches, are communistic bodies within themselves, each member rendering his whole substance to the common fund of the society, and taking upon himself the vows of poverty, chastity and humility, *i. e.* that he will have neither property, wife nor will, but will in all things accept the provisions or the deprivations ordained for him by the common brotherhood. In Catholic christianity, the highest types of religious growth are the communities, monks, nuns, and brethren of various grades. The highest type of faith is that which bends the individual judgment of each to the articles of faith formulated by the General-Commune of all the bishops. Much of the horror felt toward the Anabaptists in an early period, arose from their communistic doctrines concerning the equal right of all to the land. Accompanying the reformation in Germany, there were outbreaks of the Serfs against their Lords, based on the communistic doctrine, of the New Testament, and aiming at a more equitable re-distribution of the lands of the nobility. Simultaneously appeared a sect of Adamites, who wore no clothing and pronounced in favor of community of the sexes. The phrases connected with christianity indicate a communistic husk of origin, even where the kernel has fallen out. Thus its members are styled "communicants," a term of analogous origin with communist. The highest act of worship is "communion." The most thrilling pulpit appeals are those which exalt the duty of benevolence over that of acquisition, in a manner that if acted upon would convert the world into a christian commune, in which he who should demand one's cloak, would be kindly pressed to accept the loan of one's coat also.

There were communistic tendencies in Sir Thomas More's Utopia. Campanelli's *Civitas Solis* as early as 1623 prefigured our modern eight hour laws by a proposed law limiting hours of labor to four. In John Beller's college of industry, (1696) the laborers were to be luxuriously provided for and taught philosophy and the sciences, while the shareholders were to divide the profits. All these pale before the brilliant social dreamer, whose imagination has exercised a more potent influence than is acknowledged over modern society.

Seventy years ago Charles Fourier advanced a wild and fanciful but brilliant and seductive vision of the future condition of the world for eighty thousand years. The life of the individual, said he, must be taken as typical of the life of the race; the history of other genera of animated existence. as typical of the history of man. The individual man is born, matures, declines, and dies. Other races and genera appear when conditions are favorable, multiply, culminate, and as conditions become adverse, they dwindle and disappear. The human race therefore has its infancy—is in it now. Is it not like an infant, wholly occupied with gratifying its senses and supplying its animal wants? Only a few of any race or time have spent their lives in that which must be the mature employment of the full grown mind, in high intellectual action. These, Fourier thought, were the philosophers, statesmen, scientists, explorers, seers, poets and prophets. The average of the race have been infants. If the race after seven thousand years is still only where the individual man is at seven, then a thousand years of the world's life is equivalent to one year in that of the individual. The race will rise from infancy to manhood in a further ten thousand years. As the unit man's advance toward maturity is indicated by an increased association with his fellows, a more rapid interchange of service and ideas, and a freer association in labor and production, in government, in worship, and especially in the marital relation, so the human race, in its advance toward maturity, will be characterized by the same increase of associative power and freedom. Attractions become proportional to destinies. *i. e.,* duty is largely measured by desire. The most important factor in social science. he declared to be the relation of the sexes. If that were indiscriminate, freedom of selection being wholly on the side of brute power, the result was savageism. If it were polygamous and enslaved, the result would be a grade higher—barbarism. If it were the enforced alliance of one man to one woman, without divorce, it would be civilization, which he defined as the freedom of man and enslavement of woman. The emancipation of woman would require from three to ten thousand years, and would introduce the Harmonial Period, when the sexual attraction would be strongest in its power and most chaste, and yet most free, in its expression; when christian marriage would have passed away as identical with woman's degradation, and when, in its stead, attractions would be proportional to destinies. Instead of the isolated and solitary household, complex households would arise. A more chastened moral standard of taste and a greater delicacy and refinement of temperament would prevent these from becoming sensual, as the European and American homes admit both sexes to a larger freedom, yet with truer virtue, than those of the more exclusive Turks.

Co-operation by means of corporations and joint stock companies were also important factors in Fourier's predictions. The first experiments towards the Harmonial Relation would come in the form of easy divorce laws, co-operative communities which would fail for lack of honesty, and premature attempts at social freedom before human nature had become sufficiently refined to admit of it. The Harmonial Relation would accompany the golden period of the existence of the human race, until the whole earth were filled with the glory and beauty of a fully developed manhood, which would be reached in from thirty to fifty thousand years, after which the race would sink slowly into decay and death, the very planet becoming physically desolate.

While some of Fourier's vagaries were fantastic, few philosophers have outlined more prophetically the social drift and trend of the century that should follow them. Mary Wolstonecraft had previously asserted his doctrine in England. John Milton and Jeremy Bentham had, so far as divorce was concerned, inclined as liberally toward it as their periods would admit,

Both in England and in Germany the Protestant Reformation grew largely
out of a rebellion against the Roman doctrines of celibacy of the priesthood
and an undivorceable marriage tie.   Robert Owen, Fourier's disciple, employed a large fortune in carrying out socialism in England.   Robert Dale
Owen, son of the former, in Indiana, introduced and secured the passage of
the pioneer divorce law, which has been followed in other States, thus fulfilling Fourier's prediction.

. Most of the leading industries of the present day, in manufactures, transportation, insurance, banking, publishing, and the like, are conducted by joint
stock incorporations or financial "communes," in which the share of capital
is the integral unit considered in the government of the association, and their
owners count according to their number of shares.   The theory of these associations is the communistic one that there is perfect harmony of interests between the association as a whole and its shareholders, who, it is assumed, will
have no individual interests which outweigh their interests as shareholders.
But sometimes "rings" are formed.   The ring is a clique of officers seeking
to make more money out of salaries or contracts, by combining against the
shareholders, than they can make by acting in harmony with the interests of
the whole.   It is individualism fraudulently using the cloak of communism
to compass its ends.

Trade requires too much shrewdness, and agriculture too much toil, to be
carried on by the trustees of corporations.   These, therefore, and the mechanic
arts and professions, are left to individuals.   The individual teaches, but the
commune, called a college, gives permanency to his classes.   The individual
preaches, but the ecclesiastical commune, called a congregation, or conference,
or synod, or council, or its representative, a bishop, controls his appointment.
In art, invention, authorship, oratory, and all things requiring genius, the
individual still reigns.   In organization, and all things requiring co-operation
and numerical influence, the commune is powerful.   ,   ·

Mormonism is an oligarchic or monarchic commune, based on polygamic
fanaticism and co-operation in industry.   The Shaker communities are communes, not unlike the Essenes, based on a stoical system of abstinence, self-
denial, celibacy, and co-operation in industry.   Russia is full of communistic
villages.   The free-love communities at Oneida and elsewhere are avowedly
intended to realize the dream of Fourier, as respects property, labor, and the
complex household.   Democracy itself is a political commune as to all who
participate in the right of suffrage, and there is a communistic flavor to the
name adopted by many of our States, viz: "commonwealth."

At least a half century of democratic government was required to develop its
proper fruits.   We began our national existence under the influence of English
and aristocratic manners, habits and traditions.   We announced democratic
theories in 1776, but continued aristocratic practices, which in some degree preserved us from their immediate effect.   We continued to require property qualifications for voters, jurors and officeholders, for half a century.   We continued
the tradition that only men able to live without office should be elected to office;
that men should not seek office for its emoluments, but should wait for the office

to seek them; that judges should be appointed by the Governor and Senate; that power should not be wielded by the people directly, but through their representatives, and that statesmanship, diplomacy and government were professions requiring skill. These aristocratic traditions received their first severe blow under Andrew Jackson, and have been steadily waning since. We have become enamored of the supposed principle that all men know more than one man. We have crushed the individualism and aristocratic tendencies which gave dignity to the early administrations. In the formation of our government even the three little counties on the Delaware would not be ruled by their parent commonwealth of Pennsylvania, but must set up as a State by themselves. First, the thirteen colonies formed a league of friendship; then a confederation, having a central agency for suggestion and debate, but without either executive, legislative or judicial powers; then a union of States, in which the central government debated for eighty years with State's rights whether it were a union of States or a state of union—or as the Germans say, *Staaten-bund* or a *bundestaat;* then, by the war of the rebellion, we merged the Federal Union into a consolidated nation, which is now the sole and supreme judge, in fact, of the extent of the rights it will leave to the several States. The motto of the Republic now is, " No State shall," etc. Constitutional forms are entirely competent to say that no State shall prevent a woman from voting, or shall maintain an indissoluble marriage or the collection of debt.

Mr. John Stuart Mill, in England, so justly noted for his contempt for all the conservative forces of society, like Fourier, combined the theory that land should be the common property of all, with the theory that whenever a woman wearied of her former husband she should be allowed a change of *venue* to another. He, therefore, consented to attract to himself the wife of a relatively insipid christian gentleman of good character, and thus to prove that attractions are proportional to destinies. In America, five years ago, there were three national associations for the emancipation of woman. Their three presidents, respectively, were Henry Ward Beecher, Theodore Tilton, and Victoria C. Woodhull. The coincidence is its own comment.

We have endeavored to grasp the genius of communism, and to state its spirit and aims in the language of its more intelligent advocates, and hence in their most favorable aspect. For we regard it as a necessary and salutary force in society, when kept within proper limits by antagonistic forces. Let us now speak of its methods.

The effort to establish a perfect social commune, or association founded on the idea of the free participation of all in the fruits of its common labors, has seldom or never succeeded, except where its members have been held in union by a powerful religious enthusiasm. But large associations have been formed whose aims were partially communistic, upon less effective bases. Among these are free-masonry, and kindred orders, trades unions, guilds. Freemasonry is the guild or trades union sublimated and idealized. It began as a guild of architects and builders, in the feudal epoch,—say from the ninth to the fourteenth centuries,—and when the attractions of its principles caused nobles and gentlemen to seek admission to its order, it retained the symbols without the substance of its early functions. Doubtless, wherever large masses of workingmen have been on hire together for wages, they have combined for the common struggle against the demands of employers, and for common aid if employment failed. Our modern trades unions now number one million persons, supporting probably six millions of people in Great Britain, have upwards of half a million in France, and proportional strength throughout Europe. In Italy they were an important revolutionary factor in aiding Garibaldi to overthrow the temporal power of the Pope and establish the kingdom of Italy. Everywhere they are anti-papal, and very largely secularist. In America are at least 250,000 members of trades unions. In Chicago, at the last city election, the Socialists cast 11,000 votes; as if a city government in which but one in six of the voters are tax-payers were not sufficiently socialistic!

Most of the unionists throughout the world are affiliated with the two international associations, one aiming to control their political action, and the other to render material aid. All of them are Fourierites in their doctrines as to capital, as the following statement from their declaration at Nuremburg, in 1868, will show:

All new inventions and discoveries, instead of redounding, as now, to the benefit of the few and to the enslaving of the many, must be converted into means of reducing the toils of all, of beautifying life, and ennobling humanity. All the great, indispensable means of existence, as lands, mines, machines, and means of communication, must be the common property of all, and must be made so gradually. Nothing can reasonably be private property, but the product of labor—one's own labor.

The unions have disciplined, educated and protected the workingmen, and are of great service to them in their conflicts with capital. Unquestionably the wages classes have received far more pay in the aggregate, and maintained a condition of greater freedom by means of them. Yet, as their sole bond of union is the lack of capital in their members, they are founded on incapacity to save money, as their corner stone. Their financial theories are vagaries of the vote-yourself-a-farm-and-a-mule order, and will be until men who can save money are admitted to their councils.

Among these proletarian or wages-working classes in England, no form of communism is more significant than the creed of the Land Tenure Reform Association, which was given a prominence greater than its limited following deserves, by the fact that the late John Stuart Mill was its president and champion. This association holds that land derives its value, not in any considerable degree from the labor or capital expended on it by its possessor, but from the aggregate movements of society. The selling value of land is simply the principal on which the rent it will bring would pay the interest, *i. e.,* the value of land is arrived at by capitalizing its rental. Its rent is such deduction from the gross returns received for the products of the labor of its tenant, as the tenant is willing to make for its use. Hence all values of land are deductions from the earnings of labor. The sum which he is thus willing to deduct depends on the number of uses that compete for its possession. This, in turn, depends upon the nearness of the consumer, if it is used for production, or upon the nearness of materials, if it is used for manufacture, or upon the nearness of customers, if it is used for purposes of exchange. , All these, in turn, depend upon the aggregate societary movement, including, often, not only the commerce, manufactures, agriculture, and means of transportation of the country in which the land is situated, but also those in other countries interchanging products with that of the land in question. This societary movement makes the whole difference between the value of a vacant lot on Broadway and of one in the Sahara desert. Perhaps society ought to have some interest in the values which it thus creates, but it is difficult to conceive how such values can be distributed among their involuntary authors, who may be residents of foreign and even antipodal lands, without bringing to a sudden collapse that very societary movement through which these values arise.

In America, where we have perfect free trade in land, and only the means of transportation over it are the subjects of monopoly, the same communistic tendencies exist to regard railways, canals and grain marts as the common property of the people, as are manifested in England to "dis-establish" the private title of the nobility and gentry to land. Our railway reformers declare the railways to be public highways, and the Supreme Court of the United States sanctions the power of State Legislatures to prescribe schedule rates of freight and fare, and the rates at which grain warehouses, built by private capital, without any exercise of eminent domain or of any legislative franchise, shall store grain. Of course, American railway properties, like English lands, derive their value largely from the aggregate movements of society. But what kind of property does not? Even personal property derives its value from its vicinity to a customer who desires to use it. Of course, one portion of the public have an interest in having grain stored at reasonable rates, another portion has an interest in its storage at high rates; but no other or greater than they have in the cases of all other commodities. Thus, wherever monopoly is oppressive, human nature takes refuge in socialism. The few successful experiments in co-operative stores at Rochdale and other points in England, and the co-operative banks in Germany, and building, and loan, and insurance associations everywhere, are varied but familiar illustrations of the increasing tendency toward purely financial and industrial communism.

The theory of the expanding availability and power that co-operation may develop, is that the sole function which capital performs in business is to feed, clothe and supply the destitute laborer until returns can be received for the sale of the product of his labor—that the sole function of capital, therefore, is to cause laborers to co-operate; that this capital is ordinarily only credit obtained at the bank or elsewhere, either through the known solvency of the employer or by the deposit of the promises of purchasers to pay at some future time for the product of the employee's labor; that if the co-operation of the laborers could be maintained without capital, it would itself command the credit, which would be a sufficient substitute for the capital. All this, however, involves a greater average trustworthiness than wages workers have hitherto usually possessed. Indeed, the chief source of calamity connected with all communistic associations is, that the amount of trust required by their inherent principle of organization renders them vicious means of imposing on the unwary and impoverishing the confiding.

The secluded and private home is more expensive and less socially attractive than something like the complex household suggested by Fourier would be, if the latter were not at war with the fidelities and convictions which preserve the purity of the family. Yet, the drift of mankind, during the past century, has been towards the partial realization of the complex household, as for instance in hotel life and at the watering places. Perhaps this progress is making quite as rapidly as the best interests of society admit.

Is human progress from henceforth to consist in an increase in this power of association, until it shall work a general relaxation in the degree of individualism and exclusiveness, which have heretofore seemed inseparable adjuncts of progress, property and affection? Is the tendency to use in common large masses of property, to increase until associated masses, and finally the associated mass shall own the railroads, the mines, the manufactories and the land; until private individuals shall own, and shall desire to own, only the passing product of their labor? Is this an absolute tendency toward socialism, or is it only one of two antagonistic tendencies, and is the drift toward individualism as marked in other directions as that toward socialism is in those we have named?

If the latter be true in this country, then simultaneously with this increase of socialism there would be growing up, extending and consolidating in permanence and power, a visible American aristocracy, for only an aristocracy of some kind can make head against the inherent tendencies of a government by the non-capitalist class toward communism.

Would such a consummation be one to be dreaded or desired? On this point there is a vast amount of misconception and of communistic opinion throughout the great masses of the American people, owing to the fact that while all classes of society are pretty well grounded in the communistic theories of Jesus concerning the effect of wealth, comparatively very few look upon the subject of the accumulation of large fortunes in single hands from a purely economical aspect. No mistake in political economy can be more wretchedly stupid than to suppose that the welfare of society would be promoted by the dividing up of large fortunes or even by the diminution of the largest fortunes; and yet so commonly is this tenet held that not only those who have never amassed any large fortunes, or any fortunes whatever, but nearly every person we have met among those who have, hold almost without exception that it would undoubtedly be better for mankind, and the most benevolent act the owner of a fortune could perform would be to divide it up among the poor. This is because few persons trace out the large fortune even into its investments, still less in its economical effects. But if there were an atom of truth in this monstrous error, the robbery of the rich would be the sacred duty of the poor. But the fact is that no matter what the religion of which such a theory of property may form an integral part, it is so false that only its contemptibleness can rescue it from being criminal.

If the owner of a cart and yoke of oxen, with which he is engaged in earning his living, were approached with the argument that he ought to cut up his cart for firewood and kill and divide up his yoke of oxen for the food of the poor families of his neighborhood, he would roar with laughter at the absurdity of the proposition and would instantly point out how such a use of his wealth would create more want than it would relieve, by stopping the productive labor in which he was engaged to enable idlers to consume the capital with which it was being conducted. But the folly of the destruction or dividing up and consumption of capital so small as this, is only a little more evident, and not in any degree more demonstrable to the man who gives the subject the least thought, than would be the like sub-division and distribution of large capitals. Take for instance the $150,000,000 and upwards of capital owned by William B. Astor. Mr. Astor's ambition as a capitalist naturally is, so to manage this capital as to combine the greatest security in its investment with the largest permanent income, therefore the first requisite to this end is to keep it always in use and productive. But every productive use he can make of it is a loan in some form, of its use, to some class of persons who lack capital. So far as it consists of real estate, buildings adapted to the wants of society must be erected and maintained thereon and kept rented, and this is a loan of shelter to the homeless. The larger the fortune the less will be the time its possessor will have to find tenants, and while an owner of but few houses might, by investing his own time, rent them at high prices and on terms disadvantageous to the tenant, the owner of a large estate can only keep his buildings tenanted by keeping them more desirable than any others to be had for the same rent, and by renting them at lower rates than equally desirable premises can elsewhere be had. We find this to be the universal reputation borne by the Astor investments in New York city; all tenants preferring to hire of Astor and other similar proprietors of vast estates, and carefully avoiding the hiring of a landlord who owns but one house, provided a choice between the two is open to the tenant. Every such tenant informs you exactly what you would infer from a slight reflection, especially if your judgment was guided to its conclusion by the very simple principle in political economy, viz., that the smaller the quantity of time which a landlord can give to his investment, the lower the rate at which he will be compelled to make it, and that the capital of a large capitalist never averages but a small fraction of the ratio of interest per cent. that is expected by a small capitalist. Of course if the Astor estate were distributed among as many owners as there are tenants, there would be a general advance of rents among all the tenants, and the charity would thus result in an immediate tax upon industry to sustain idleness.

A. T. Stewart, by selling ten times the quantity of goods that had previously been sold by one merchant, was enabled to reduce by nearly nine-tenths the fractions of cost which had previously entered into the selling price of goods to pay for store rent, service of salesmen and the like. He might therefore take off four-tenths of the difference between the buying and selling price, and still make a profit five times greater, *on his own time*, than his brother merchants. Thus in no mode would his capital so speedily, evenly and judiciously divide itself up among the poor, in the form of reduced prices on goods, as by leaving him to manage it in the manner which would most promote his own wealth. The massive stores, shops, factories and other appliances which he erected are virtually the property of mankind in their essential utilities. That which Mr. Stewart substracted from all his wealth as the net compensation for superintending its amassments, consisted of the food he ate and the clothes he wore; probably not exceeding $1000 a year. Even his marble palace and paintings are the property of the world as truly as is the shell that encases the coral. insect after the worker has shrivelled in death. When Commodore Vanderbilt determined, for the better preservation of the estate he had amassed, to practice the English system of primogeniture by leaving nearly his entire wealth to his eldest son, he taxed the world with the expenses of one system of management only in preference to five or six. If subjected to competition, the cost to which William II. Vanderbilt can, if necessary, reduce the expense of management of $200,000,000 of capital invested in railways will be the sum required for the support of his one family. If not subjected to competition, it must be because no other capitalists believe they could loan to the public an equal amount of capital, or the capital necessary to compete with him, at so low a rate of profit as he is doing. In either case the public are being served at the lowest possible rates.

The secondary economies growing out of the "luxurious living" which is attributed to the possessors of large wealth is generally very little investigated or understood by the "sell all thou hast and give to the poor" school of economists. All luxury is involuntary but highly economical charity, simply because all the articles of luxury, not being articles of necessity or indispensable, are not produced by the competent or well conditioned class any where, but by the extremely and precariously poor, who, but for luxurious living, would be crowded out of existence. Food, shelter, clothing and hardware being necessities of life, are in such ready demand at remunerative returns, that the well to do business classes in all parts of the world who can select the more profitable occupations, everywhere are engaged in furnishing them. But laces are knit, and diamonds are cut by the poorest classes of artizans in Paris. Pearls are hunted by the humblest fishermen of Ceylon. Furs are gathered by Kamtschatkans and Esquimaux on the frontiers of polar cold, where humble life struggles feebly against the eternal chill. Diamonds are sought for by the hungry beggars in the mountains of Peru and Hindoostan. Even gold and silver hunting are the resourse of the shiftless and adventurous class, while coal and iron are mined by wealthy corporations that endure for scores of years and even centuries. Raw silks are the products of the labors of the almond eyed Mongols, who work at a penny a day, and the Hindoos, whom the most untiring industry fails to rescue from famine. The weavers of silk are nearly their counterparts in France. The grapes for the finest wines are cultivated by the peasantry skirting the bases of the Alps and Appenines, and the roses from which the finest genuine perfumes are extracted bloom on the blood-stained and tax-drained fields of Albania and Bulgaria, where for centuries the cross has maintained its unequal contest with the crescent. So, traversing the entire range of luxuries indulged in by the very rich, we find they have sent relief in some degree and at some distant point to the exceptionally poor. The real waste and loss to society diminishes as we ascend, and dwellings, furniture, clothing, all the incidents of life, become more durable in proportion to the substantialness and elegance with which they are constructed. The least costly element present at a royal wedding are the Queen's diamonds, for the wear of them for a thousand years would detract nothing from. their weight, brilliancy or value. The expenditure incurred for them was not a consumption or loss of wealth, but a mere investment, which the nearest jeweller will cash on demand as a banker would a note. They are not the subject of waste. But the boots and hat of the outriders in livery, that accompany her carriage, will wear out in a few months. In like manner the least costly thing connected with society is its aristocracy, for nearly every expenditure made by a capitalist is a permanent investment, while most of the expenditures of the peasantry are for objects which disappear in a few months, or at most years. And of all the elements of an aristocracy, the most economical are ranks and honors: for they are a species of payment for public service, which secures more consideration and respect from the masses than can be purchased with money; are, therefore, of more value to the possessor than wealth, and yet cost the public treasury and the tax-payers absolutely nothing. In our universities and armies we retain and dispense ranks, titles and honors as the reward of merit, and no people are more proud of them. It would be safe to say that including political, scholastic, military, legal, medical and clerical titles, we have at least one million of titled persons in America. To each of them his title, whether it be Col., Rev., Dr., A. B. or Hon., is as dear to him as a very considerable share of his fortune. The differentiation of society into many grades and ranks is as inseparable to the highest efficiency of the sociotary movement, as its differentiation into occupations, sexes, sects, and schools of opinion.

The necessity of recognizing aristocracy in all societies increases in proportion to the inequalities of condition and development which mark the social life. It is far greater in American society to-day than it was a century ago, greater in the cities and towns than in the rural populations, and has always been greater at the south than at the north because the south brings side by side an inferior race upon whose minds the rudiments of industrial civilization are barely dawning, a class of degenerated whites who know little of politics in the higher sense of the term, and an educated landowning class who have been accustomed to look upon the two former classes very much as the Roman patricians looked upon the plebian dependents of his *gens*, or as the feudal baron protected, patronized or plundered the serfs of his clientage accordingly as they were loyal and deserving or rebellious and treacherous. The Southern States, from the beginning, developed their gentry and their peasantry. Probably either the colored race must be eliminated, or the white race must cease to contain any representatives of the *ancient noblesse*, which, during the first fifty years of the republic, rendered that section the ruling one, before Southern society can cease to be aristocratic in a sense much more fundamental and determined than most of the people of the North can conceive. The great reason why the weight of Federal despotism rests oppressively on the South is because it is the despotism of the principle of democracy which, in the true sense of that word, the South despises, over that of aristocracy which the South loves. There will never come a time, during the next two hundred years, when it will not conduce to the best interests of the South to be governed by her aristocracy of educated landholders, rather than by her democratic rabble of negroes and poor whites. The political alliance, therefore, which the Republican party of the North undertook to form with the negroes of the South, who being the illiterate mob, are, in the sense we use the terms, the democratic party of the South, *i. e.* the party of non-taxpayers, was illogical and could end only in misfortune and failure. It was as ill advised as the alliance existing before the war between the Democratic (Irish) vote of the North which was largely non-taxpaying, and the aristocratic slaveholding party of the South.

The true interests of both sections require such a re-adjustment of parties as will cause each State, county, town and hamlet to contain its balancing elements, its two parties; instead of allowing whole towns and States in one section of the Union to swing into one party, to be only off-set by towns and States voting solidly against them, a thousand miles away. The latter condition tends as irresistibly toward civil war, as it did before slavery was nominally abolished.

No fear need ever arise of any dangerous consequence to result from conflicts between the tax-payers and non-tax-payers of the same town, county or State. Being face to face with each other they will be compelled to talk the matter out and come to an understanding, Each has certain rights in government, and in the true analysis the interests of capital and labor are harmonious. But that this harmony of interest may appear, it is essential that both be heard through their authorized representatives.

The representation of capital in both the Northern and Southern State legislatures would supply a balance wheel in our constitution, which would lessen the hatefulness of the Union to the people of the South, because the Union would then come to recognize those aspects in which men are unequal, instead of onesidedly recognizing only those aspects in which they are equal. So long as capital punishment is practiced it is the sheerest folly to maintain that all men have an equal and inalienable right to life. So long as imprisonment for crime prevails it is equally silly to assert that the right to liberty or the pursuit of happiness is either equal or inalienable. Human rights are graded in every State according to the aggregate judgment of that State. Local self-government consists in permitting this difference of judgment to prevail. They will differ most widely where the capacity for their right exercise is most unequally diffused. So far as any system of Federal law may seek to break down the aristocratic distinction between the white race and the black at the South, it will come into conflict with a law as much more irresistible than Federal law, as the law which controls the circulation of the blood is more irresistible than the law which controls the impounding of stray cattle or the sale of meats. Republics have the same right, under the constitution of the United States, to be aristocratic that they have to be democratic,—to maintain inequality in the rights of citizens as to maintain equality. The constitution requires every State to have a republican form of government, but does not require any State to have a democratic form of government, nor that its social customs shall recognize social equality. In so far as the power of the Federal Arms has been brought to bear to convert the aristocratic republics of the South into democratic republics, it has not succeeded, and never deserved to succeed. This fact will continue to make itself manifest in the social life of the Southern States, and it is the part of Northern statesmen to recognize the legitimacy of the aristocratic principle in republics, *i. e.* of the rights of capital as against mere numbers.

By giving representation to capital, they can at least erect a bulwark against its further abolition, for the same force of numbers that could abolish slavery could abolish banks, corporations, credit, and even distribute the lands by a majority vote. The capital of the North, which was so freely poured out to abolish slavery, may find that its sorcery hath raised a spirit which will not down at its bidding.

What South and North both especially need, and without which they can not long be held back from another civil war, is, that such questions and policies shall be brought before the country as will break up the two sectional and passionate mobs called "parties," which are now drifting us all hopelessly toward another war, and shall compel a conflict in which large masses of influential men in each section shall unite politically with equally large masses of influential men in the other.

Such a question would be the re-organization of our State governments, in such manner as to give capital or the tax-payers a distinct veto on the action of the non-capitalists, and the re-organization of the National government, so as to render the Executive and Cabinet responsible to Congress, and Congress responsible directly to the people, which can only be effected by the system of resignable ministries and dissoluble legislatures set forth in chapters I and II of this pamphlet.

If it be said that the agitation of two such questions, and at once, would rock the fabric of our political society to its very centre, would divide the upper classes of society against the lower, the poor against the rich, and the property-holding against the non-property-holding, then my answer will be, so much the better, for only in this way can past issues be sealed up in oblivion, the union of the States preserved without war, the Cæsaric despotism of section over section be ended, a new holocaust of a million lives and a thousand millions of treasure be averted, and the Republic lifted into a dignity, as to its constitution and destiny, worthy of its dignity in point of numbers and wealth.

These being the premises upon which I venture to believe that an appeal to the American people in behalf of the re-organization of our constitutions, both State and National, should be entertained, it will be perceived that I am not searching after Utopian excellences merely to satisfy the cravings of an æsthetic imagination. I am not seeking to gild the refined gold, nor to paint the lily, but to avert an impending appeal to arms, which, without constitutional reconstruction at the North as well as at the South, is inevitable, and which, if it comes, while it can not be more unnecessary or perhaps more bloody than that through which the country has but recently passed, will prove even more unfruitful of results that are consistent with true republicanism or with human welfare.

Shall we be told that the war, by abolishing slavery, has removed the cause of war, and, therefore, that we are secure against its revival? This argument has three fatal defects: *First,* that slavery is not, save by the continued maintenance of a degree of Federal intimidation, which is inconsistent with State freedom, abolished. *Second,* that the class of prophets who now predict that there will be no war because slavery is abolished, is the same which, prior to the previous war, predicted that war could not result from the passionate treatment of the slavery question, because the South would foresee its abolition as the necessary consequence of war. As prophets they stand impeached, from lack of familiarity with the Southern mind. And, *thirdly,* the prophecy assumes that people never go to war without a good cause, whereas the converse is true, that people seldom go to war *with* a good cause.

As regards the abolition of slavery, we have, it is true, a constitutional amendment, providing that slavery and involuntary servitude, "except in punishment of crime," is abolished. But what a Trojan horse is the exception. Each State can define crime, and slavery in punishment of crime is as lawful as slavery as the consequence of race ever was. Moreover, there is no law preventing the Southern States from excluding the blacks from holding office, for although the XIVth amendment provides that no State shall make any law which shall abridge the privileges or immunities of citizens of the United States, yet the courts, Federal and State, have, in an uninterrupted score of decisions, held that this language, which occurs in a previous clause of the constitution and in the ordinance of 1787, does not include the "privilege" of holding office. It is easy to see that, on the withdrawal of Federal authority from the Southern States, the control of the matter of slavery in them is relegated to State control, and that the Federal government is in control of no machinery for reversing the action of the State, except war.

Under these circumstances, it was earnestly to be desired that as soon as possible after the physical rebellion was crushed, the intellectual and moral rebellion of the southern people should also end. The more sagacious leaders of the Republican party of the North, viz: Lincoln, Seward, Chase, the Blairs, Sumner, Trumbull, Julian and Greeley, labored to this end, and were, one by one, crucified by the relentless bigotry and stupidity of the rank and file of their party, who looked upon every attempt to heal the breach occasioned by the war, as treason to the Republican party, and every recognition of the right of the Southern States to that equality of rights which the North had fought to maintain them in, as being a defeat of the northern arms. The attitude of the North and South, which might, by the prevalence of wiser counsels, and by passing on to new issues, have been converted into one of fraternity, has been, instead, congealed into one of disarmed neutrality and sullen dislike.

The peculiar manipulation by which a probable popular verdict in favor of Tilden was transformed into an electoral verdict in favor of Hayes, was not cured by the surrender by Hayes of the "Republican" cause in two of the States whose electoral votes were counted in his favor. ·It was looked upon rather as the act of the thief caught "with the manour" upon him, throwing away that portion of the plunder which was to form the share of his confederates, only to facilitate his escape with the share which he himself would enjoy. The effect of this peculiar course of politics is, that the issues which the war should have settled are not settled. The success of the Republican party, and the revival of the Democratic, at each ensuing election, has rendered it necessary to re-open them, according to that peculiar crab-like genius, which pertains to our system of voting, as explained in chapters I and II, whereby we must, of necessity, vote on past issues.

It is totally immaterial in which section, or from what causes, or by whose fault, or in which political party, the elements of this incapacity for self-government originate, so far as its effect to precipitate the republic into disaster, and prove the incompetency of the aggregated whole for self-government, is concerned. The experiment of a republic in America assumes that the people, as a whole, of both sections and of both parties, are fit for self-government. If this assumption is false as to half, it is false in all. If the North could prove that the South is unfit for self-government, the same proof would convict the North of the same incapacity; for, if the South were unfit to be a partner in the firm, why did the North compel the continuance of the partnership? ·Mutual recrimination, therefore, like reciprocal vilification, only establishes the incapacity of both parties.

The prospect before us is far from satisfactory. Great as have been the sacrifices which the people of either section have made in the interest of what they supposed would promote their future welfare, the country now presents every indication to the calm and thoughtful mind of being once more adrift in the rapids, tending downward toward another civil war. One thing Americans may as well understand, bluntly and at the start. If the American people, as a whole, of the North as well as of the South, have not, for any reason whatever, the capacity to organize politics so as to avoid the formation of two sectional political parties, one of which shall represent the "solid South," and the other the "solid North," then the American people have not the capacity for self-government, but out of sheer passion and stolidity are doomed to drift out of one civil war into another, until the very heart and life of republicanism are extinguished in military despotism. The politics of the country can not be run by the solid North against a solid South, from decade to decade, without the recurrence of periodical civil wars, resulting either in the establishment of permanent Cæsarism of one section over the other, which would be an abolition of republican liberty, or in separation.

Possibly we have not the materials for creating an aristocracy after the European pattern, in which pride of inherited fortune, honor and reputation often outweigh the pride of personal character, achievement and ability. It may be reserved for us to demonstrate that European aristocracies have very crudely and imperfectly represented the influence which capital and culture should have over government. Possibly, however, we are to be always confined to the weakness of a government by the unskilled. It would be to us a new and high ambition to seek to illustrate the machinery by which capital, experience and culture may be given their due share in the control of a government, without recalling the ballot from any to whom it has been given.

We will not say that ranks and titles are to be created. Even in monarchies many men of the highest rank regard these as baubles which could not add to their dignity or estimation. But it may well be doubted whether ranks, honors and titles are not at once the most economical, satisfactory and useful modes of rewarding public service and giving distinguished recognition to merit. However this may be, we do need the habit of dignity which ranks and titles have promoted, or our civilization itself will be overslaughed in vulgarity and smut.

There are essentially but two forms of government in the world, viz: a government by the better classes, and a government by the worse classes. All appearances or pretenses either of a government by one man or of a government by all men, are equally delusive and false. As large a ratio of the people are employed in the work of governing in Russia, which purports to be government by one, as in the United States of America, which purports to be a government by all. True, in America the people may change their governors at stated intervals, and in Russia they can not. But to change one's governors is not to govern. The ruler, whether he be a monarch or a majority, must represent either the aristocratic or the democratic class. The best government will balance delicately between the two antagonistic influences, swinging wholly into the control of neither. The aristocratic class will bring to it wisdom, integrity, pride of birth, character and fortune, experience, conservatism and the influences of culture, art, veneration for all that is worth preserving in the past, and personal and official dignity. .

The democratic classes will bring physical vigor, readiness to change, hardihood, inconstancy, turbulence and revolution. Athens, Rome, Venice. Germany, France and England all laid the foundations of their greatness during the ascendency of their aristocratic class. Assuming that the experience of nations justifies the doctrine, that in every government capital as well as labor, experience as well as ignorance, and the honorable as well as the lower classes should be represented, it remains to consider how this should be done. In England and throughout Europe a peer casts one vote in the House of Peers, whether his possessions are great or small, and in some cases even though they may have been dissipated or squandered by his fault. This, after all, is a class representation and not a representation of capital. In the recently proposed charter for the city of New York it was provided, that the Board of Finance, or upper branch of the city legislature, should be voted for by taxpayers only, but there was no provision whereby the power of the tax-payer's vote should be proportionate to the amount of taxes he pays. This also is a representation of tax-payers as a class, but not of capital as a force or power.

' If capital is to be represented with any accuracy in government it must be by providing, not only that the upper branch of the state or city legislature shall be voted for by tax-payers only, but that such elections shall be held at a different time, upon a different registration, and by the use of totally different machinery from those at and by which the popular branch of the legislature is chosen. Each voter must be registered as entitled to cast a number of votes proportionate to the capital he owns or the taxes he pays—say one vote for every ten or fifty dollars of taxes he pays,—or to be more accurate, for every dollar of tax so paid. Every legislative district, being first alloted its quota of members of the upper house proportionate to its assessed property, will choose its number of members on the same principle as directors are chosen by the shareholders in a corporation, *i. e.* if the district is entitled to three members, then the three candidates receiving the votes representing the largest value of assessed property will be elected, and the persons voting for either of the defeated candidates will have the power within a limited period to transfer their votes to either of the elected candidates, so that their voting power shall not be lost. Presumptively, therefore, the three members elected will hold the proxies of all the tax-payers in their county. However that may be, each member will cast in the legislature the aggregate vote of the tax-payers whom he represents. Some slight actuarial labor will be rendered necessary to count the vote rendered in this manner, but the result arrived at will be, what no government has ever yet so perfectly obtained, viz: a representation of capital. Under such a system, corporations should vote through their officers as if they were individuals, and women as freely as men, in the election of the capital branch of the legislature in question.

It might also be provided that well certified intelligence, especially on political topics, should increase the voting power of the citizen, in the upper branch of the State legislature, though its possessor were not a tax-payer. If one extra vote be given for every fifty dollars of taxes paid, then let one who has been three times re-elected to any town office have one or two extra votes, as may be adjusted, since this continued approval furnishes as sound an evidence of his superior experience and intelligence as would be furnished by his accumulation by his own industry of property paying fifty dollars a year of taxes, or thereabouts. Let a third re-election by the people to county, state and federal offices increase the voting power of the citizen in an ascending ratio, in electing the upper house. Thus, if a vote is regarded as equivalent to fifty dollars of taxes paid, then one who had been twice a State Senator or Representative might have two extra votes, and two more for each second additional re-election. One who had been twice a Representative in Congress might cast ten extra votes, and ten more for every third re-election. One who has been twice a Judge of the Circuit Court might cast five votes, and five more for each third re-election. A Governor or United States Senator should cast say twenty-five votes, an ex-Vice-President fifty, and an ex-President one hundred votes—only, of course, in the election of a member of the upper branch of any state or city legislature. Service for five years in the army might entitle to an extra vote, with an increase for officers. Members of the legal profession should cast three votes, and those who had completed a classical course in any college in which constitutional law and political economy were taught might cast one extra vote. The details of the plan are immaterial so long as the principle is preserved that the three elements of Capital, Experience in government, and Intelligence or Culture, are to be represented as accurately as a Constitutional Convention in its wisdom may be able to provide.

At present, neither in our state nor city governments does the boasted and vaunted division into two houses serve any useful purpose whatever. The two being chosen in the same manner, represent the same elements and interests and are duplicates of each other. But if one represented heads only, and the other chiefly property and intelligence, they would efficiently offset each other and check the drift toward a government by the worst.

The views here presented are essentially identical with those advocated by Mr. Calhoun in his "Essay on Government," except that he confines himself to the statement of a principle in constitutional government, while the foregoing proposition seeks to supply the mechanism which will apply that principle in practice. Mr. Calhoun's principle is, that all governments by mere numerical majorities, are governments by ONE FORCE,—*i. e.*, by that majority,—and hence that they tend toward absolutism, it being only necessary that the majority party shall delegate their powers to, or submit to their usurpation by, their chief, and the government forthwith becomes in effect a monarchy; and even without this delegation it is always a despotism, governing by numerical force, and not by compromise. He holds that government, to be enduring, must be a compromise between different *estates and interests,* each having a veto on the other. This he styles a concurrent majority, *i. e.*, a concurrence of two majorities—the majority of numbers, and the majority of wealth, or whatever the other represented interest may be. A government by concurrent majorities alone deserves to be called constitutional. All governments by mere numerical majorities are absolute, and not constitutional. He instances Rome, where the plebian interest or estate, through its tribunes, was given a veto on the action of the patricians, and *vice versa;* and Great Britain, where capital in land is represented in the House of Lords, and the numerical majority in the Commons. In the city government of Berlin there is a systematic effort to represent capital in the upper house of the city legislature.

Of course it will be assumed by the inert class of politicians that no law which lessens the relative power of the non-capitalist masses, compared with that of the capitalist class, can now be passed, since it will require the favorable votes of the very class whose power it is designed to diminish. Certainly the measure must be calculated to secure the votes of the majority of existing voters. But after due agitation a plan could be devised essentially on the foregoing principle which would secure the votes of the majority of existing voters. The number whose power of voting would be increased by the above plan would probably exceed half the total number. To these add the large number of candid non-property holders whose sympathies are so far with the property holding classes that they would vote for what they thought would take the governing power away from the incompetent, whether they themselves would have their voting power increased or not. Few men are more conscious of the contemptibleness of rabble government than the men who participate in it. They are, as a rule, more willing to admit their own unfitness than the more educated and responsible classes are to assert it. By all these means the power to remodel our constitutions in the interest of a due and proper representation of capital, and so as to secure for it a far more adequate and just representation than it has ever before had, is to-day within the reach of the capitalist classes, who, I believe, will be found to be the majority of all voters.

. I would not, by such or any means, seek to overcome the just and natural expansion of that principle of association which finds its highest and most marked manifestations in the various forms of communism. I would only seek to place side by side with it a principle which is to it what the masculine is to the feminine, what the positive is to the negative, what law is to liberty, what science is to mystery, viz: its better and truer half—its more perfect self.

www.ingramcontent.com/pod-product-compliance
Lightning Source LLC
Chambersburg PA
CBHW031453270326
41930CB00007B/978